Praise for *C*
Walking t

"Manifests in a moving way th. ....p .... between the inner and outer journey of the pilgrim, and all those who engage lovingly and intentionally with the practice of walking meditation. Guide[s] both those who are beginning to practice, as well as the mature practitioner.... Provokes deep reflection and stimulating insights for the reader."

—**Sheryl A. Kujawa-Holbrook**, Claremont School of Theology; author, *Pilgrimage—The Sacred Art: Journey to the Center of the Heart* and *Hildegard of Bingen: Essential Writings and Chants of a Christian Mystic—Annotated & Explained*

"In the companionship of treasured soul friends and with breath drawn through words and walking, small practice pieces release a spacious wholeness. We are generously welcomed to experience this spiritual expansion again and again."

—**Rev. Dr. Martha Brunell**, spiritual director, writer, retreat leader, pastor

"A lovely book built on walking from [what] is to what should be. This book ... should be read."

—**John Mark N. Reynolds**, PhD, president, The Saint Constantine School; editor, *The Great Books Reader: Excerpts and Essays on the Most Influential Books in Western Civilization*

"Part poetry, part prayer, part adventure, part meditation ... this beautiful invitatory opens wide the doors to explore inner and outer worlds with equal curiosity and soulful guidance. Count me in for the practice of *camino divina*!"

—**Betsey Beckman**, founder, The Dancing Word

"[This] fascinating alt-guidebook arrives at a singular historical moment—one in which the field of cognitive neuroscience and neuro-aesthetics has begun to bring a robust, evidence-based musculature to bear upon the rather ancient practice of pilgrimage…. Indeed, the scientific literature showing the connection between physical movement and increased creativity and wellness is growing every year…. It sounds almost silly—but in an era when a pharmaceutical answer to every ailment seems all too readily at hand … the science and fact of a simple walk, accompanied by a guidebook like [this] may be the only thing one needs to open up vistas of the imagination, attuned to the promptings of the world, the miracles of discovery that lay before us with every step."

—**Mark Svenvold**, assistant professor of English,
Seton Hall University; author, *Soul Data*

WITHDRAWN

Camino Divina

Walking the Divine Way

A Book of Moving Meditations with Likely & Unlikely Saints

GINA MARIE MAMMANO

Walking Together, Finding the Way®

SKYLIGHT PATHS®
PUBLISHING

Woodstock, Vermont

Camino Divina—*Walking the Divine Way*
A Book of Moving Meditations with Likely and Unlikely Saints

2016 Quality Paperback Edition, First Printing
© 2016 by Gina Marie Mammano

All rights reserved. No part of this book may be reproduced or reprinted in any form or by any means, electronic or mechanical, including photocopying, recording, or by any information storage and retrieval system, without permission in writing from the publisher.

For information regarding permission to reprint material from this book, please write or fax your request to SkyLight Paths Publishing, Permissions Department, at the address / fax number listed below, or email your request to permissions@skylightpaths.com.

"Becoming a Begging Bowl on the Sacred Path to Chimayo," on pp. 16-19, was originally published as "A Moving Meditation on the Sacred Path to Chimayo: 'I Am a Feather on the Breath of God'" in the August 2014 edition of *Connections*, published by Spiritual Directors International, www.sdiworld.org.

Library of Congress Cataloging-in-Publication Data
Names: Mammano, Gina Marie, 1965- author.
Title: Camino divina-walking the divine way : a book of moving meditations
    with likely and unlikely saints / Gina Marie Mammano.
Description: Woodstock, VT : SkyLight Paths Publishing, 2016. | Includes
    bibliographical references.
Identifiers: LCCN 2016003774| ISBN 9781594736162 (pbk.) | ISBN 9781594736292
    (ebook)
Subjects: LCSH: Spiritual life. | Meditations.
Classification: LCC BL624 .M327 2016 | DDC 242—dc23 LC record available at http://
lccn.loc.gov/2016003774

10 9 8 7 6 5 4 3 2 1

Manufactured in United States of America
Cover Design: Jenny Buono
Interior Design: Tim Holtz

Walking Together, Finding the Way
Published by SkyLight Paths Publishing
A Division of LongHill Partners, Inc.
Sunset Farm Offices, Route 4, P.O. Box 237
Woodstock, VT 05091
Tel: (802) 457-4000 Fax: (802) 457-4004
www.skylightpaths.com

for Rick and for Margaret

Contents

Introduction

What is *camino divina*? Well, since *camino* simply means "road" and *divina* means "divine," the pair of them together could be thought of as "the path of the Divine" or "the divine way." It's a merging of the Spanish *camino* and the Latin *divina,* a lingua marriage of sorts. In my vernacular, it just means taking a meaningful stroll out in nature, on a labyrinth, under the moon, with divine words laced in rhythm along with it.

I was walking a pilgrim path in New Mexico on the road to Chimayo when I realized something helpful and quite beautiful: small bites of ideas can slowly, deeply nourish the soul. I can hold on to a handful of wise words and take them in as a whole meditative meal, but I can also enjoy them individually, berry by berry, word by word. It was a bit of a revelation. On that walk, I took a phrase I had long loved—held in my memory box for years—and then plucked it, slowly, slowly, word by word, so that the sweetness of it went much further than the usual reading. Instead of gulping the whole phrase down, I let each part of it roll around in my mouth, in my soul, drawing out each flavor.

I asked myself, "What does this first word say to me? What pictures do I see? How have I defined this word in the past? How do I fling the past as far away from me as I can, and see the word in a totally different light? How can I play with it, fiddle with it in my mental 'fingers,' and from it fashion a whole new collection of meaning for myself?"

As I practiced this simple exercise, walk by walk, place by place, I realized that it not only enriched my walking practice but also drove rich meaning deep down into it. I was *savoring* the berry, rather than choking it down whole, really tasting the subtleties of texture, form, and flavor in each word I moved with. My walks were becoming more than walks; they were becoming a way into the Divine.

As a spiritual director and a person trying to live life lovingly and intentionally, I find the constant challenge for myself these days is to "slow down, slow down, slow down and redefine." Redefine my words, rename my thoughts, tenderize the tough and thick understanding of things that I've held on to for years. Find new ways to see the old wineskins, pour newly fermenting words into new word-skins. In life, each person's experience is unique. My nuance is not your nuance. My story palette is not yours. The meanings of words I take along in my life-lesson hobo pack do not hold the same mementos that yours do. And time adds its own set of refinements. My nuances of word and wisdom have changed dramatically over the nearly five decades I've lived on the planet, and I'll bet many of yours have, too.

The Journey Ahead

This book is designed to take you on a journey—no, many journeys—of both outer landscape and inner landscape. The outer landscapes are all around you and can be explored through a well-planned or serendipitous trip, a pilgrimage to a sacred site, or a meandering somewhere in your own neighborhood. The pith, though, is found in the inner landscape. That is something you take with you wherever you go. It is your inner self, the very soul-housed uniqueness of time and space that you bring into the world and bring into your life's experiences.

I've created twelve adventures that give you the chance to traipse into both of these realms—the inner landscape and the outer landscape. On each adventure I've paired you up with a spiritual guide whom I call a "saint"—a sage who has spoken inspiring words and ideas into my soul and out into the world. I've then chosen a theme that highlights one aspect of the featured sage's wisdom and legacy, but by no means encompasses it. As you wander into themes like Amazement, Wildness, Darkness, the Liminal, the Surprising, or the Familiar, know that they can be explored not only with the saint associated with that particular theme, but with the others as well, serving as launching points for you to explore many other possibilities in your *camino divina* practice. When you've finished this book, I encourage you to create a list of your own "saints," those whose words and thoughts have inspired—and continue to inspire—you.

Each chapter begins with a very short biography of the featured "saint." This is a chance to whet your whistle for the first time or rekindle an old friendship with the purveyor of wisdom chosen for that chapter. I give you just a pinch about his or her life and a taste of how I got to know this word-wise sage as well.

Next you will find a reflection on a *camino divina* journey I've taken—an outer landscape adventure that I've invited my own inner landscape to come along with. This portion of the reading is an invitation for you to step into the forest of "the way of the Divine" and get a taste of the journey as my open-eyed companion. It also provides some helpful examples on how to walk the divine way with an open soul and open hands and how you might journal about it afterward.

The next section is a "sitting meditation" focused on the spiritual luminary of the chapter. This is a beautiful opportunity to take a little time out to ruminate on the soulful gifts this saint can bring to you as you take him or her on your *camino divina* journey; it also simply gives you an opportunity to breathe, to rest. I find the things that seem to stick best to my soul and nourish me in simple, slow release are the ones that have a chance to percolate without strict margins of time and expectation, though I know we all have them. With this in mind, I encourage you to read the sitting meditation through, then take a few moments of quiet. Then read it again, pulling from it desires of the rich spiritual gifts you most want for yourself. Then sit in quiet again, taking into yourself your own hopes for both growth and appreciation for what already lies inside you.

The sitting meditation is followed by a *camino divina* adventure. This is your chance to amble amid a place of your own choosing, your own landscape, with the same words, the same phrase I took along on my *camino divina*, but adding your own textures, nuances, life flavorings to the basket of words you will carry with you. You will notice that some of the adventures focus on individual words spoken by the luminary of the chapter, while others savor sounds and the way they flavor a thought, and yet others take on the meditation of a whole phrase at a time. There are many ways to relish the wise words presented here. To help these resonate with you, I have created some questions, ideas, and ponderings to take along the way.

And finally, each chapter closes with a section called "The Longer Walk." Within it are opportunities that allow you to take your *camino divina* journey beyond the first treads, by playing with "What Is Found" poetry, taking a "Deeper Dive" into the saint's words, and expanding your experience through group gatherings on "The Scalloped Path."

However you choose to use and reuse this book, my hope is that you journey into this world with your inner and outer landscapes synchronized, aligned, attuned to the divine delights, insights, and challenges awaiting you with each and every word. Happy walking!

Why Walking Meditation?

Two states and a few mountain ranges away from my native southern California, I found myself in northern New Mexico at a basin dip in the sun-soaked landscape, hugged by sweet, red-tinged mountains, when I saw … *it*. The labyrinth. *Wow*, I thought to myself. *This is so cool! A labyrinth … now what do I do?* I proceeded to quietly approach the red clay serpentine formation, that silent coil of mystery, and remembered someone saying, "When you enter it, make an intention." *OK, I can do that*, I whispered. I think mine was something like "May I know more about myself by the time I am through." Yep. Simple. Not really specific, but honest. I started walking, dare I say tiptoeing, onto the rich red road. I held my intention—loose, lightly formed, and unspecific as it was—and walked. And walked. And walked. And as I walked, I breathed. Breathed more thoughtfully. And not just breathed; I felt an opening in my chest. Ahh. I felt space and roominess in the place where my own lump of pulsing aortic clay, lodged inside my heart cavity, might begin to have a little wiggle room. And *wow*, my mind opened up, too. Questions started gently flying in like silk scarves from a laundry line when subtle winds knock things loose. *What do I already know about myself? … What more would I like to know? … Where would this "I" like to go next? … Do I need to think about it? Or just feel it out … intuit it … let my gut lead me? What does it feel like to do that? Should I try it on for size?* The little pistons in my legs continued to chug along, allowing the Rube Goldberg mechanism of blood to heart, blood to brain, air to lungs, wingspan in soul to armspan in body to continue to connect, snap in place, flap, move, exhilarate, think, and click. Walking meditation. That's all it was. On my little labyrinth, in my moment, under a blue wispy sky, like a little, pulsing, rib-caged bird.

All along the people and place continuum, far beyond novitiate attempts at first labyrinth experiences like mine, folks do walking meditations for all sorts of reasons, and it's been going on for a long time. The famed Santiago de Compostela walking meditation pilgrimage—a five-hundred-mile or so path that originates in one of many places on the European continent and concludes in Galicia, Spain—began around twelve hundred years ago with a pilgrim seeking the remains of a beloved apostle. Over time, it became for many, in the words of British explorer Sir Walter Raleigh, "a scallop shell of quiet" along the roads of their own inner lives. It didn't start out that way. In the thirteenth century, it was the hustling, bustling, many-peopled way to walk out the swerves, curves, and sand traps of the spiritual life, or "the way of Christ," in microcosm. Along the way, seekers welcomed hardships, hospitality, and tests of faith as a picture in miniature of the soul's journey, rather than having to make the distant trek to Jerusalem or Rome, and picking up an indulgence or two along the way. For many today, it has become a meditation adventure into rich, juicy metaphors of the life journey. These may include allegories of the soul's solitary walk, the surprise party of companionship, nature as rugged and delicate partner, and communion with spirit within and Spirit without. In other words, walking meditation.

On a different continent, within the rich realms of another spiritual tradition, walking meditators on the island of Shikoku, Japan, have been connecting the dots of about eighty-eight separate shrines and temples via foot and shoe for hundreds of years, taking the 750-mile mountainous route, up and down, round and about, as it metaphorically follows each stage on the path to nirvana: awakening, austerity, discipline, enlightenment, and, finally, nirvana itself. Locals there follow the custom of *Osettai*, as they offer "charitable giving" through food, accommodations, and other kindly practical gifts given to the visiting meditative walkers—another hospitable version of the welcoming scallop shell found by happy seekers on the "way of St. James," or the Camino de Compostela in Spain. I might add that this one is not a walking meditation for the faint of heart or the frail of body, as it is said that pilgrims of old starting out on the Shikoku pilgrimage donned white burial jackets, as the trek was long and dangerous, and they felt they must be prepared for anything, even death.

And less formal versions of walking meditations have gone on for centuries. A great chunk of John Muir's life was one big walking meditation, as he traipsed through the Yosemite Valley, thinking mountain cathedral thoughts like this:

Climb the mountains and get their good tidings. Nature's peace will flow into you as sunshine flows into trees. The winds will blow their own freshness into you, and the storms their energy, while cares will drop off like autumn leaves.[1]

Walking meditators today, who find themselves near San Francisco or the Pacheco Pass, may choose to follow in his footsteps and walk the "Muir Ramble," a great open meditative opportunity to let the earth teach them what it will. In Muir's words, spoken as he rambled about,

... we had plenty of time, and proposed drifting leisurely ... by any road that we chanced to find; enjoying the flowers and light, "camping out" in our blankets wherever overtaken by night, and paying very little compliance to roads or times.[2]

Yes, it takes many forms, this "divine way" of walking.

And there are many reasons people of all sorts meditatively walk. Some do it for clarity, abandoning the gush and rush of everyday life, hoping to replace it for a while with *cohos*, zephyrs, and winds of change. Others do it for reflection, a chance to reenter the motion pictures of their minds in order to re-create coherent story lines and begin new ones. Some seek self-forgiveness— the shoulders of granite above them and the arms of rivers below them holding a space for pain and transformation. Some look for internal healing from a past or a present rife with question marks, dancing and prodding them to engage the mystery, then allowing for the sweet surrender of self-care and solace. Others want understanding. An openness to the cosmos. Connection.

The road does not have to be long to be meaningful. A short hike, with engagement and intention, can be packed with rich insights and rewards that can be cherished and reflected upon for days. A "sacred site" does not have to be listed in a fancy travel book or on the UNESCO World Heritage website to be authentic. It can be wherever your booted or sandaled feet take you—the entrance to a local forest or preserve, a walk along the water, a well-focused trek around your city or neighborhood. Meaning is what *you* bring to the experience. Place is where *you* live it. My walking meditations have been as lofty as the pilgrimage to Chimayo and as humble as a stroll through a local park.

What Is the *Divina* Connection?

Long ago, I fiddled with *lectio divina* in a small church group gathering in a high school basement. From the little I had read about it, it sounded like a cool idea, a "feasting" on sacred words:

> First, the taking of a bite (*lectio*); then chewing on it (*meditatio*); savoring its essence (*oratio*) and, finally, "digesting" it and making it a part of the body (*contemplatio*).[3]

Yum! As a confirmed foodie, I really liked the idea of ingesting tasty things, whether on the plate or on the page. Words, tumbling around in my mouth, feeling out the syllables and the sounds, then relishing all the possible meanings—their historic definitions and my own personal clusters of connotation—was a delectable alternative to just taking them in, gulping them down, or swallowing them whole.

I dug *lectio divina*. It gave me a chance to make a word, a phrase, my own. It allowed me to listen deeply to Self and Spirit. It afforded me the opportunity to suck the juice out of a text, extract the pulp from beyond the pulpit. It gave me freedom and space. It gave words incarnation.

Some time later, when I was in a flurried frenzy to know more about *lectio divina*, I discovered *visio divina*. Oh, and the gears were cranking, the newly oiled thoughts were ticking. *What!? A practice that allows a person to feast on art and contemplation? Where? ... How? ... What have I been doing all these years?* So I checked out this tantalizing practice. I borrowed some books by British art critic and contemplative nun Sister Wendy Beckett. I scoped out great online sites and I sat with the works of the great early sixteenth- and twentieth-century painters Raphael and Paul Klee for blissful moments of time out of time. The colors and images were rolling around in my mind, in my soul, nourishing me in as wonderful a way as the *lectio* version did.

Now for the *divina* connection. Simply put, *lectio divina* literally means "divine reading." *Visio divina* means "divine seeing." My own internal connections and discoveries led me to create the term *camino divina*, or "divine walking." The larger expression of this has been practiced for years through pilgrimage and walking meditation. The specific expression of it emanates from my own desire to savor poetry, wise sayings, and other "sacred texts" that have been pulled into my own life book from well-loved, well-respected sources in order to "walk out" a new way of feasting on words.

What Is a Spiritual Practice? Why Engage in One?

As some of you may already know, "spirit" comes from the word *spiritus*, or "breath," in Latin. In Hebrew, it's *ruach*. So when you're trying out a spiritual practice, you're literally trying out a new way to breathe. You're creating an opportunity for yourself to absorb the air all around you in expanded and open ways.

And "practice" really means not getting it perfect, at least to start. It is a grand and messy experiment to explore the art of finding out who you are and where you belong in the world and possibly beyond. When I let the word "practice" have a little space and flexibility around it, words and phrases like "daily custom," "deeper dive," "dance with soul," "commitment to Self and Spirit," "imperfection," "incarnation," and "inspiration" show up. I think, in some ways, "practice" has gotten a bad rap in the last several decades. Instead of the free-moving airways that a good, healthy practice can foster, for many people its nomenclature connotes "stiffness," "unbending ritual," or "mindless rote." A sad, lonely punishment for such a good word!

There are many ways to engage in a breathable habit, as I like to call it. Spiritual practices may be as historic and intricate as hatha yoga or Ignatius Loyola's daily *examen* and as simple and straightforward as feeling gratitude or engaging in intentional acts of kindness. My spiritual practice table-spread has included things like journaling, contemplative reading, praying out loud (my morning verbal ramble), nature walks, group spiritual direction, embodiment prayer, and community art experiences. And no! I've never done all of these at once! Whew! I think it would be a course in hyperventilation, rather than healthy "breathing." Sometimes the practice cycle for me is quarterly, monthly, weekly, or daily. And sometimes, it's skip-a-daily. The idea is breathable habit, with an emphasis on "breathable."

But habit, no matter what form it comes in or what span of time it takes up, can be a good thing, a very good thing in the case of spiritual practice. It's a pattern. A rhythm. Just like breathing. You count on it every day, every moment, to literally *in*-spire you, give you life. That's what a spiritual practice can do, too.

How Is *Camino Divina* Different from Other Forms of Meditation?

The twentieth-century mystic and faith healer Saint Pio of Pietrelcina once said, "Through the study of books one seeks God; by meditation one finds him." Information alone can never bring about true relationship—with the self, with the Divine, with the natural world, with anything that's a living, knowable entity, and I mean that in the continually unfolding sense. To get to *know*, you have to *get to know* in the personal-space, meet-for-tea-or-coffee face-to-face, get-down-to-the-juicy-conversation kind of way. It's all about personal experience and engagement. For example, I can tell you all day what a strawberry is, but until you actually taste one, bite into the uniquely formed, sweet redness of that particular ground-growing berry, you won't be able to wrap your head around the fullness of what it is. It will be equated with "sweet" and "red," making it just as easily an apple, a cherry, or a vine-ripened tomato.

So meditation over the centuries has been a way to practice finding the true essence, in the Saint Pio sense. Of course, it has many other iterations as well, including developing compassion, emptying out the mind, releasing the past, and focusing on the present. I love a couple of the Hebrew words associated with "meditation": *haga*, "which means *to sigh* or *murmur*, but also *to meditate . . .*"and *siha*, "which means *to muse,* or *rehearse in one's mind*."[4] Sounds so human, doesn't it? Sighing, murmuring, and rehearsing when it comes to the sacred art of meditation.

Camino divina, as a form of walking meditation, encourages the practitioner to sacredly run amok with word associations, imagination, histories, and enlightenings that emerge during the walk. As in other forms of meditation, we're engaging in a deep and focused listening, alongside deep rivers of acceptance and freedom. The ears of soul attuned to the voice of memory, the voice of story, the voice of intuitive impression, the voices of nature, the voice of "self," the voice of God or Spirit, and, of course, the voice of the poet, the writer, or the likely/unlikely saint highlighted on the walk. In this practice, you are given the opportunity to discern for yourself what meaning-making can be sculpted out of the clay of place, physical movement, and meditation, incorporating the surprise gifts opening up all around and within you, both praiseworthy and puzzling.

How Do You Practice *Camino Divina*?

The only ingredients you need are a string of wise words, a chosen place to walk, and a deep determination to be true to who you are at *this* moment, and to *that* place you intend to walk around in. Once you're holding that handful of fairly "simple" things, take a deep soothing breath and step out your front door. Then just start moving.

I suggest keeping the writer's phrase in your head, memorized, or jotted down on a piece of paper. That way, you can refer to it over and over again. Let that phrase melt into you as much as possible. It may take many readings, and it may stick in your throat, rather than melt, but that may be good, too. It may pose an interesting challenge to work through as you walk your *camino*.

As you're beginning your walk, be sure to take in the smell of the world around you, whether it's ocean air or the subtle remnants of highway exhaust. And look around you. Take an interest in particulars. Instead of noticing a familiar object, notice the *texture* of a familiar object, the *ombre* of it as it graduates from dark shade to lighter shade, the subtle colors inherent in it, the creatures or people who may live inside it. Attempt to be open to sights, sounds, feels, or smells that you normally wouldn't be.

Then, look again at the likely or unlikely saint's wise phrase, picking out and focusing on just the first word. It may be a word you've seen a hundred times on its own, or a word you just don't like, but take a look at it. Repeat it in your mind. If you can, feel the contours of the sound and shape of the word. Let it have its own dignity as a lettered form of expression. Say it again. What does that word remind you of? What stories, situations, events, readings, places, personal histories does it conjure up? What does it remind you of in the context of *this* place? Do any new thoughts or insights come to mind with *that* in mind? Where are you now … on your walk? … Where are you now … inside this word? Where are you now … as you ponder the interactions between these things? Now, check out your environment again, the place where you are walking, and take *that* in. Move on to the next word, along with the next steps on the path, and let it all unfold.

As you peruse the chapters of this book, you will notice that I begin each one by sharing my own *camino divina* experience. I walk the line, holding my own copy of the saint's words, sharing with you my own impressions, wonderings, connections, and histories. This may spark something in you as you begin your walk or just help you feel that you have a companion on the road of being human.

Even though we take the same phrase along our different walks, we take it into different places, with different people, *you* and *I*, making each of our journeys completely unique. Consider me your friend and guide along the way.

The Longer Walk

Deeper Dive

To dive even more deeply into the words of a writer or the thoughts of a sacred wisdom keeper is quite valuable. Walking widely in the world of the sages is helpful, but plunging more deeply into the rivers of only one can be a rich experience. This gives you the opportunity to excavate treasures embedded in the depths, which are much harder to see when you're only scratching the surface of things, and that endeavor is well worth the extra time and engagement. To assist you, in each chapter I've provided some additional savory phrases by the highlighted saint. I've chosen each one with the spirit of an additional *camino divina* adventure in mind. I recommend taking an extended excursion with one or two of them, and, in doing so, spending some extra moments with an author off the beaten path. As you choose which phrase you'd like to take with you, you may want to think of these words as rosary beads, held intentionally and thoughtfully, delightedly connecting the visible world with the not-so-visible.

"What Is Found"

I used to love creating "found" poetry. My best memories of this are when people shared their journal entries out loud after a day of immersing themselves in the "book of nature." I would write down their most memorable lines and phrases, the ones that stood out to me for their beauty, their impact, their uniqueness.

After they finished, I would pull together the chosen words and phrases from their work and create a "found poem" out of them. I would assemble the lines, phrases, and words fairly loosely into a quick free verse poem, invariably reflecting the heart of their journal entries. It always deeply touched me how amazed each person was at their *own* words once they were taken from the oyster shells of their longer journal ruminations and held up to the light, illuminated individually like pearls.

As you will see, after each adventure, I have included my own pearls written in the form of found poetry. I do this in order to share with you the beauty and power of how further reflection after a *camino divina* journey can become crystallized into potent ideas, thoughts, and feelings, emerging into a memorable gem.

Of course, I encourage you to create your own found poetry from your *camino divina* walks, highlighting the best of what you've experienced. If you've recorded your experience in your journal, you can start by underlining words, phrases, or lines that jump out at you—the ones that especially strike a chord, or elicit a picture, a life lesson, or a memory. Once you've done that, write them down on a separate sheet of paper in their original order or in a form that pleases you. There are no rules here. Play with it a little. The key is to find the gems within your own treasure trove of writing and recollecting, then display them for your own remembrance and enrichment.

The Scalloped Path

On the Camino de Compostela pilgrimage mentioned earlier, the scallop shell symbol is a significant one. Besides a harbinger of hospitality, displayed prominently on houses and inns, it also represents the many starting places people come from on this well-trod journey. Each of us walks our own path, as from the edges of the shell's own outer grooves, moving all the way down to a central meeting place at the bottom. The convergence of pilgrims on paths like these mirrors the convergence of grooves on the shells.

The deep symbolism of the scallop is described further by a recent pilgrim, who says:

[The shells] came in various forms: ceramic shells fitted onto road markers, government-issue traffic signs marked with an abstract shell, shining brass shells embedded in sidewalks. Some were broken, some had been stolen as souvenirs, leaving only a trace of their presence, some were beautiful, some so simply sketched as to provide the mere suggestion of a shell. In all their variations, they marked the route for hundreds of miles. They reminded all of us pilgrims that in the midst of a world both beautiful and broken there are signs to help lead us forward, sometimes right under our feet.

In each chapter, "The Scalloped Path" gives you the opportunity to enrich your *camino divina* experience by meeting up with other pilgrims along the way. Included are some enticing questions and opportunities to share your experiences and insights. I find that the reflection and the retelling can be almost as valuable as the adventure itself. And hearing others' inroads into the outback of interior realms and exterior landscapes can add value and depth to your own experience.

As you reflect together, it's fun to think about practicing the "code of hospitality," which was common in most ancient cultures, and is still practiced on many pilgrimages today. For the host, it includes treating everyone who enters your door with respect. For visitors it involves doing the same toward their hosts, treating them with great respect as well as offering to be helpful whenever possible.

Chapter 1

An Adventure into the Familiar

Wendell Berry—Prophet of the Soil of the Soul

Fed and watered among the soils of Henry County, Kentucky, Wendell Berry has nourished readers and rooted himself deeply in the causes of earth and community for more than four decades. His reach in the world extends from the rich word-scapes of novelist and poet, to the fertile landscapes of environmental activist and cultural critic, while his feet remain firmly planted in the furrows of Lane's Landing, the land he's farmed as neighbor to his own family's historic acreage since the mid-1960s. David Skinner, in a well-crafted biographical essay on the the National Endowment of the Humanities' website, puts it this way:

> Whether in a verse concerning a yellow-throated warbler perched on a sycamore branch, or in his fictional stories of the people and times of small-town Port William, or in his essays discussing the dangers of erosion and pollution, there are several constants:

admiration for nature's ingenuity, respect for locals
and local knowledge, and a deeply Christian appreciation for our obligations to each other.[1]

Some may say he has an affinity for front porches and
"home" landscapes, but think of them both as multi-
layered and multidimensional architectures of the soul
and soil, digging deeply into the value of generational
wisdom and thrusting upward into the hopeful skies of
preserving our futures. He is noted as saying, "Essential
wisdom accumulates in the community much as fertility
builds in the soil."[2] As a writer, an activist, and a person
of faith, he wears boots caked with commitment. From
rallying against the poison of coal ash to lamenting the
destruction of rural communities through soil loss and
toxic pollution, he has put his pen where his heart is.

My own connection to this richly composted writer
came initially through his poem "The Sycamore," a
beautiful and intricate ode to the tenacity of this tree.
In my memory of that first read, I am slowly rambling
though the poem until I get to this line and the ones that
follow it: "It has risen to a strange perfection / in the
warp and bending of its long growth." There is a catch
in my soul, a stunningly bittersweet but grateful sense
that the story of the sycamore is the story of the self—a
long history of growth and injury, wreck and repair; a
connection to the raw scars of this broad-leafed senti-
nel healing over and over and over again. The words of
Wendell Berry, the environmentalist poet, novelist, and
essayist, have now taken root in me.

Walking the Woods in Ordinary Time

"The search withholds the joy from what is found."
—"Boone"

There is a little loop trail on Craw Road within the curl of Whidbey Island, where I live—a dollop of forest tucked next to the main highway. This could be considered just a simple county park. I've never seen any more than three cars parked in its stale gray parking lot. My pilgrimage today is for my body and for my soul. I'm physically tired, so a whim of a walk feels just right. Nothing too long, nothing too fancy—a quick picnic on an interior journey.

This loop doesn't go far, but I know it goes deep. I've walked it before. For its tiny tuft of real estate, it drops a person into a thicket of trees—tall, stately spindles lined up together that leave no more room than a few small slivers of sky. It is a cold place, even on a sun-filled late spring day.

"The search withholds the joy from what is found," Wendell Berry tells us in his poem "Boone." *The search*. What has been my search? I search, and I search, and I search all the time. Every day becomes a deeper delving into nooks of ideas, ponderings, hoped-for probabilities, possibilities, and preferences. And the bigger questions always rise up, too: What is the purpose for my life? How can/will I get there? Why do I feel the damp dankness of darkness sometimes? Why is there darkness? Can we learn to see through it? Is it as bewilderingly beautiful as some people say? As frightening? Who lives there? God? Is God in the darkness? Who is God? What is God? Will I find teachers to show me these things? Can I be my own teacher? What is it in spring leaves that makes the sunlight seem more than sunlight? Why so much complexity in a carpenter ant? Why the expanse of a thousand or more invisible universes?

I search. I search. *The* search. *The* search. The search *withholds*. A conundrum, taking all this time to roam the astral planes of thought and spirit; I thought the search would open up a glimpse into the answers. Open up the hidden passageways into my own soul. How does the search *withhold*? What does it withhold?

I am now deeper into the forest. It is a large swath of straight lines, a blur of wooden twigs, bark, and needles. A large, cool darkness. A continuous repetition of species. I stop. Hush.

A noticing takes place.

Trees now, not forest. This is what I see.

This one is smooth and pale, slender like an early moon, holding on to a wisp of sunlight on its woody skin. This one is a grand monument. Its craggy furrows are spun with moss and web, a somehow mansion for a kingdom of creatures that are each under a centimeter in length. This one chirps with a pair of battling birds, a nuthatch and its nearly invisible adversary, vying for the gentle weave of sticks and lighter flora that have fallen from above to make a nest.

And now, I hear. It sounds like an ocean where I am. A large swelling wave of sound. There is no visible wind. I am far enough away from the highway to simply dismiss it as the whoosh of cars. It sounds as if something very large is speaking. As if I'm holding my ear to the seashell of the Universe. I don't know what it is, but it is big. I can't tell what it is, but it is here, in my midst.

The search withholds the *joy*. What joy?

I see the winding movement of a nuthatch scaling up the tree like a tightrope walker, a small player in an impossible carnival act. I imagine the seashell of heaven, opening up its pearl-pink curl of clouds so I can wonder, press my ear up into what the trees are saying. I watch the long, brushstrokes of pines making a winding spiral of endless curiosity deep into the acres of loam. I feel my body, walking smoothly, limb and limb into scent and sound, suddenly, unexplainably refreshed. The joy.

Of what *is*. What is. Myself. Age forty-eight. Alive. Able to walk this trail today, inside and out. The sun. Lighting up the sky and my mood after three days of rain. The forest. Dark, cool, preserved. I don't have all the answers. I do have what is *found*.

I have found so many things thus far inside my own life. That friends make my life habitable. That beauty in all its nuance and variation is in itself, just because it *is*, worth adoring. That stories are worth listening to, taking in, swallowing, savoring, digesting, then deciding whether to store or release them. That life is a daily manna, abundance is only from sunrise to sunrise. That security is in a constant hide-and-seek game with the pleasures of risk. That *the search withholds the joy from what is found.* This is the treasure hiding within the folds of the present moment. This is the surprise waiting to be discovered under a sky leaved with confetti and forested with ribbons of sound. This is the forever reward wrapped in final recognition. This is *what is found.*

Likely or Unlikely Saint?
A Sitting Meditation

"And the world cannot be discovered by a journey
of miles, no matter how long, but only by a spiritual
journey, a journey of one inch, very arduous and
humbling and joyful, by which we arrive at the
ground at our own feet, and learn to be at home."

—*The Unforeseen Wilderness:*
Kentucky's Red River Gorge

I had a friend stop me in my mental tracks once and say these words to me: "The search withholds the joy from what is found." I was ready to have them tattooed on my forehead immediately. Within the nest of this conversation between us, we shared the tangled struggle of trying to figure things out, untie the many knots of the universe and ourselves.

"Wow! I love and admire you so much, but you seem to spend so much of your time wrestling with so many things" was the gist and grist of what my friend said to me. And then came Wendell Berry's words from his lips: "The search withholds the joy from what is found."

I felt something unlock in my soul. What have I already found? Can I enjoy each ribbon of knowledge or experience without tangling them all up into a knotty stew? Can I slow down and marinate in some gratitude for the things I already know? The things I already am? The things I have already lived out?

The answer is, "Yes, I can." And, I can also continue to search, but may it not take up so much of my life, so much of my time that it "withholds the joy from what is found."

I picture Wendell Berry, this prophet of the soil of the soul, holding a stone in one hand, a mineral metaphor of "what is" and "what is found." It starts out at his feet but then is picked up and noticed.

And I imagine the crumbling loam of a well-composted life flaking off in his palm in the other hand—"dirty" hands, well lived, well loved.

I want this for myself, too, and so I pray, and so I say: May I be a prophet holding the stone of what *is* in one hand and the rich soil of my own well-composted life in the other … and know the joy of *what is found*.

Amen.

Camino Divina Adventure: Into the Familiar

It is time for your own adventure, your own foray into the wise words of Wendell Berry, mixed and mingled with the deep wisdom of the self. All you need is a place to walk and the phrase "The search withholds the joy from what is found" to take along with you.

Where you walk is up to you, but I would recommend somewhere not far from your home this time around, as this is an adventure into the familiar. A local or regional park could work, your own backyard, the Euclidian grid of the neighborhood right outside your front door, or the yawning street-lit walks of your town or city at sunrise or sunset.

Go slowly (and safely). Measure your steps. Take each stride as an opportunity to be fully present to what is around you—those places you see every day on the way to work, to the grocery store or farmer's market, to a friend's house, walking your pet, picking up a family member—but perhaps never really notice. Take in as much as you can around you. Notice the simple. The easily ignored. Think about questions like these as you walk: What do I see? Does a crack or bend on the path of a familiar sidewalk look different during this time of day or does it look unerringly familiar? Is there a beauty to it? A curiosity about it? An unknown history? What could that be? What is the lovely peculiarity of that ordinary plant that's been growing there on the side of the road as long as I've passed by here? Do I know what it's called? Has it changed over time? Where else have I seen its kin? What do I associate with it or the places where I've seen it grow? Memories? Feelings of like or dislike? Now, in this moment, if you listen more intently, can you hear the audible shades of sound from the cries of a small child to the piercing caw of a crow? What other sounds do you hear? What other sounds do you barely hear?

As you're walking, try to take each word separately from Wendell Berry's line "the search withholds the joy from what is found." Play with every one of them on your tongue and in your imagination, eyeing and adoring them individually, like small children, even the too-familiar words like "the." Hold them in your thoughts for a moment or two. Playing and savoring are key. Ask yourself questions like these: What do I associate with this word? What have I never noticed about it? Where does this word show up in my life over and over? Or why does it rarely show up? Then walk with it. Go on a scavenger hunt, trying to collect familiar thoughts and ideas that resonate with that word. Then collect new ones. Remember, take it one word at a time, step by step, while also remaining aware of what is around you. Without and within. Let the walk take you places where you've never been, even though it's really taking you places where you've always been.

Finally, ask yourself: What have I already found as I've walked my years on this earth? What joys might be gleaned from this finding? And what is "the joy from what is found"—this hour, this breath, this moment?

THE LONGER WALK

Deeper Dive

Digging more deeply into the rich soil of Wendell Berry's words may take you into territory undiscovered, yet once uprooted, plowed, and harvested, somehow familiar. Just like his Sunday morning walks along his beloved Kentucky farmland, you may want to make it a habit to try a *camino divina* walking meditation regularly, starting with one or more of the lines below composed of Wendell Berry's well-composted words. Here are a few more phrases you may want to walk out:

> Practice resurrection.

> To be healed we must come with all the other creatures to the feast of Creation.

> Love is what carries you.

> The impeded stream is the one that sings.

> Accept what comes from silence.

"What Is Found": Into the Familiar

> Loop trail on Craw,
> a dollop of forest,
> a preserved whim.

> Nothing too long,
> nothing too fancy.

> "The search withholds …"

> deeper delving—
> the nooks, the hoped-for, the bigger questions,
> why the expanse?

> Hush.

> An early moon, a somehow mansion,
> the gentle weave of sticks,
> a swelling wave of sound.

> "the joy …"

Nuthatch scaling,
limb and limb.
Life is a daily manna.
Folds of the present moment.
The forever reward.
The seashell of heaven.

This is "what is found."

The Scalloped Path

Walking a meditative walk like a *camino divina* can be an experience greatly heightened by the companionship of others in story and afterglow under the welcoming seashell of someone's living room, sacred community place, or gathering space. Here are some questions for further exploration with fellow path-taking pilgrims after experiencing an adventure into the familiar.

1. Did you have an intention when you began your walk or your "search" or was it more spontaneous, serendipitous? If you did have an intention, what was it? What may have prompted that intention?

2. Where did you choose to walk? What drew you to that place?

3. What word or words on your walk really stood out from the poetic line, "the search withholds the joy from what is found"? Did other important images, concepts, or memories unfold alongside this word or words?

4. What did you notice in your outer landscape? In your inner landscape? Anything surprising? Anything

profound? Anything seemingly simple but somehow deeply affecting?

5. Did you find yourself "searching" so much on your *camino divina* that the search withheld the joy? Can you tell what you were searching for? If so, share it as best you can.

6. Did you find joys on your walk? What were they? Describe one or two in deep and delightful detail.

7. Did you find anything unfamiliar about the "familiar" place you visited and thought you knew so well? What did you notice? Why do you think you noticed it today, now?

Suggested Readings

Berry, Wendell. *The Long-Legged House.* Berkeley, CA: Counterpoint Press, 2012.

A collection of essays that exemplify his words: "What I stand for is what I stand on."

Berry, Wendell. *This Day: Collected & New Sabbath Poems.* Berkeley, CA: Counterpoint Press, 2014.

A chance to step with Wendell Berry on his thirty-five-year-running every-Sunday Sabbath walks and enjoy "what is found."

Berry, Wendell. *Traveling at Home.* Berkeley, CA: Counterpoint Press, 2011.

Included is Wendell Berry's essay, "A Walk Down Camp Branch," a foray into the familiar.

Berry, Wendell. *The Wild Birds: Six Stories of the Port William Membership.* New York: North Point Press, 1989.

An entryway collection into Wendell Berry's celebrated series of novels, which include *Nathan Coulter, A Place on*

Earth, The Memory of Old Jack, Hannah Coulter, and *Jayber Crow*.

Berry, Wendell. *Window Poems*. Berkeley, CA: Counterpoint Press, 2007.

Early poems through the eye of his forty-paned writing studio window, looking out and noticing the natural world.

Chapter 2

An Adventure into Wonder

Hildegard of Bingen—Mother of Verity and Viriditas

Hildegard of Bingen, the eleventh-century, tenth child of a German noble family, is aptly called a polymath. This little-used word comes from the Greek term *polemathes*, which means "having learned much," and implies internal access to a very large body of knowledge. It is little used because few people have ever lived up to the vastness of it. Hildegard, of course, is one of the exceptions. Here's why.

She was an abbess, philosopher, poet, biographer, composer, musician, mystic, artist, preacher, playwright, doctor, herbalist, botanist, theologian, architect, and, to some, an early practicing naturopath. And if that's not enough on her curriculum vitae, she was an inventor of an alternative alphabet, called *Litterae ignotae*, or translated into English, "unknown language." Charles Moffat, in his article "Hildegard of Bingen: The Biography of a Feminist Nun," published in *The Feminist eZine* in 2002, states:

Hildegard is credited with inventing opera. She endorsed beer drinking for the nuns because she believed the drinking water was not safe and it gave them a rosy complexion. She invented her own coded language.[1]

A true pre-Renaissance renaissance woman, if ever there was one.

Like many others of the spiritually curious, I continue to be intrigued by Hildegard's visionary images that bear names like "Cultivating the Cosmic Tree," "Universal Man," and "All Beings Celebrate Creation," alongside musical compositions titled, "O Most Splendid Gem," "Loving Tenderness Abounds for All," "O Ruby-Red Blood," and "O Luminous, Shining Mother."

I'm not sure where I first found Hildegard of Bingen: trying to learn about labyrinths and stumbling across the word "viriditas" for the first time as I wound my way through? Glazing past the "fiery cosmic egg" somewhere in an art book or while sailing through cyberspace and needing to stop for a second or third look? Or sitting with a very wise woman who once said to me as I was feeling anxious about my next steps in life: "Be a feather on the breath of God." However it happened, whether between a book's cardboard covers, floating mystically out in cyberspace, or falling from the lips of my first spiritual director, wherever I found this visionary, this "Sybil of the Rhine," I'm grateful and glad I did.

Becoming a Begging Bowl on the Sacred Path to Chimayo

"A feather on the breath of God."

—From a letter to Odo of Soissons, 1148

I am not alone. We pilgrims stop along the dusty road that leads to the sanctuario de Chimayo, wind licking and tickling aspen trees, cottonwoods. I straggle behind a bit. I decide I will hold a bowl made of fingers and palms to see what God drops inside. I am that hungry for what may be. I will see what my begging bowl provides for me.

A few steps on the path, I look down at a pile of crunchy flora, creating what looks like yellow confetti at my feet. I pick up a handful. Now the bowl is filled. "I am a feather on the breath of God," I whisper. Within minutes, the wind gladly pulls my confetti away. The sky is bespeckled with golden circles. I watch in delight.

I find the bowl is now empty again, begging.

I spy a yellow dandelion, a small sun among its crop of siblings, accompanied by its own razor-edged green leaf, beautiful in weedy simplicity, more than the genus we've relegated it to. It glows in my hands. As I continue to walk, I approach something quiet, something profound, and the *descanso* emerges, a flower-bedecked memorial site. I enter its space with reverence. A life was lost here. It is decorated with the colors of love and sunset, bouquets of longing and desire. I place my small, soft, yellow contribution on top of its cross. "I remember you, too, though I didn't know you," I say deep inside as the dandelion glows, a yellow dot among the tokens.

My empty bowl in front of me again, I wait. I walk. I am "a feather on the breath of God."

In time, below me, I see a small stick; its smoothness attracts me. Are mine the only hands that have held this? I don't think so. I am now this tiny tree's human companion and its former holder is mine. Not long after it rests among the branches of my fingers, I notice a creek, moving in clarity, small but determined. I throw the stick into it with serendipitous glee. Where will it go? Where will it end up? Where will I? I am "a feather on the breath of God."

"No," I repeat slowly, "*I* am 'a feather on the breath of God.'"

I am here. *I* exist. *I* am *I*.

Grateful for this revelation, *I* move on.

"I *Am*." I then whisper, feeling inspired, "I *am* part of this magnificent Divinity. I *am* part and I *am* whole. I *Am*. I *am* part of the Great. I *am* part of the I *Am*. I *am* 'a feather on the breath of God.'"

I walk a bit farther, each word of Hildegard's phrase tumbling out with more meaning, more savoring, as I remain present with it.

I spend some time in wonder, then I say, "*a* ...," small, humble. A little word, a little me, among a sea of Being; among a landscape of beings. I am *a* ..., one of many; one of One.

"I am a *feather*." The wind kicks up. I am shifted, lifted in the delightful feeling of floating, imagining myself white like the down of a mourning dove, lightweight, tickled by the fingers of an unknown presence. I don't care where I go. It is enough to drift with the wind, to be carried by unseen joy.

"I am a feather *on* ..." I continue. My feet are suddenly heavy. Clay on clay. Grounded. Human. Immediately grateful for being earth on Earth. I am human. I am here. I look down. Path and feet are united. "I am *on*."

When the time is right, I lift my gaze from the ground beneath me and anticipate the next word: "I am a feather on *the* ..." Usually such an inconspicuous word but now it holds the Great Mystery. *The*. It is the place of Unknown. It is solid yet indecipherable for me. It is the great Namer, yet without a Name. It holds the place of something beyond itself.

I keep walking and then I move on. "I am a feather on the *breath*."

The Breath is all around me. Moving trees are swaying under its influence. It is lifting leaves and dropping them on rockways and walkways. Writing its own poetry.

I breathe. I draw in the deep drafts of living. I realize the begging bowl is now within, filling with oxygen. And then, I remember *ruach*. The name for the Holy Spirit and for *breath*. Holy Wind. Breath Wind. Circulation of

Life to and through all beings. I am caught up in the circulation. Out-breath and In-breath. World-breath. Life-breath.

"I am a feather on the breath *of*." Yes, *of*. I sense a calling of direction from the east, the movement of wind from another place toward where I stand. *Of* denotes origin. Now it denotes gift, brought to me from some other distance. It is in my hands, it is on my body.

"I am a feather on the breath of *God*." Silence. Awe.

This last word is too large. How can I take it all in? If I swallow it, certainly it will swell out my fingers, burst through my rib cage, and forever flow, leaving my body behind in a helpless melt of surrender. If I attempt to capture it in words, surely it will escape my grasp and whisper slowly outward, seeping over the mountains, away from everything in glorious mystery. How can I say, how can I know, this one last mouthed moment on my pilgrim journey?

"I am a feather on the breath of *God*."

It is too large. I wait. I wonder. I form a figure of human silence …

I now know. I myself will be the begging bowl. I will let go my fingers, my cupped hands, and I will open myself, clay spreading outward on the wheel, whirling wider, arms spilling westward, eastward, feet rooted in the soil, chest pointing up to the sun. Empty.

Then Filled.

Likely or Unlikely Saint?
A Sitting Meditation

"There is a power that has been since all eternity
and that force and potentiality is green!"

—Wax plate engraving, twelfth century

Hildegard of Bingen is a bona-fide, beatified saint. She shows up on these pages because she is a wonderfully strange one who doesn't fit the mold of what many of us think a saint looks or sounds like, or at least what I think a saint looks or sounds like. She is a composer of songs. A creator of pictures. A cauldron of ideas. Her vision is in brimming, light-infused Technicolor. She is a vibrant woman who created her music as "The Harmonious Music of Celestial Revelations," not as a slow-glowing form, frozen in time with dusty gold-leaf halo and three fingers held up al fresco.

The word "viriditas" is associated with her, "a word meaning vitality, fecundity, lushness, verdure, or growth, often as a reflection of the divine word or as an aspect of the divine nature."[2] She used the word as a symbol of physical and spiritual health, the force of life behind life, holding and moving through it with vitality. So to bring her words along on a forested trail; in a sweet, green, carpeted meadow; or to any lush, natural setting just seems, well, natural.

She is quoted as saying,

The soul is the greening life force of the flesh, for the body grows and prospers through her, just as the earth becomes fruitful when it is moistened. The soul humidifies the body so it does not dry out, just like the rain which soaks into the earth.[3]

Now that's beautiful, verdant, and truly "viriditas." Roll that idea around in your soul for a while.

When I picture this already "sainted" saint, I envision her in lush robes of meadow green, velvety and soft, moistened with the moisture of the soul, while allowing life's circumstances to carry her on a warm breath, empowered by Love itself.

I want this and so I pray, and so I say: May I be a "greening" human being, able to feel the verdancy of my own humanity, who is moistened by the rain of my own soul, and carried like a feather on the breath of God.

Amen.

Camino Divina Adventure: Into Wonder

You are wandering into the fields of wonder today. Every niche, every nook is an opportunity to gaze and consider, notice and appreciate, ponder in your heart, hold in your hands. To be a "feather on the breath of God" is to be open to where Spirit Wind takes you.

For this adventure, I'd recommend starting out by taking a few moments to close your eyes and just breathe. A mini-practice in *noticing*. Notice the ebb and flow of taking in and letting out, the rolling pattern of expansion and retraction in the chest, the warmth or coolness of the air you're breathing in. Then, a mini-practice in *wondering*—wonder at the subtle sounds around you, right in the place where you're standing or sitting. Listen. Then feel the tension or relaxation present in your own body. Notice the very space around you, the layers of sight, the layers of sound, the layers of *feeling.*

Once you've taken the time to warm up to wonder, recapturing the simplicity of your own availability, openness, and presence, you're ready to begin holding each moment that waits inside the phrase "I am 'a feather on the breath of God.'"

And as you venture out today, try to imagine yourself as a begging bowl. Back in the day, dating historically to the Buddha, the Franciscan friars, and beyond, certain holy men and women chose, and still choose, to allow themselves only a small bowl and perhaps a simple wooden spoon to hold their daily supply of nourishment. This was called a begging bowl. Whatever appeared in their bowls, be it a helping of rice or a serving of soup from a kind stranger, or a ladle of cool water from a well along the way, this was the gift and the provision given, and it was accepted with gratitude, believing that enough was "as good as a feast."

What would it look like if today, on your *camino divina* walk, whatever came across your path became an unexpected gift placed inside your begging bowl, the begging bowl of your being? It might be a creature showing up in nature, a thought or an idea swirling into your mind, or the serendipitous presence of another human being walking along the path as well. How can you take it in as a thing of wonder? What words would you use to describe its sudden appearance along your walk? What words would you use to describe each one as a gift?

The key to this experience is receptivity. What gifts may come floating into your inner life through your outer life today? What will capture your attention, captivate you, take you onto the rabbit trail of experience? In nature, in found objects, in weather patterns, in darkness and light?

As on all the adventures, try to be in tune with your inner landscape as it plays with your outer landscape. After you've allowed yourself to become grateful, to open as a begging bowl, try to take Hildegard of Bingen's words one at a time, like found fluffs of feather down, collected one at a time, and allow each one to take you somewhere. Somewhere unexpected. Sometimes it's the meaning of the word, sometimes it's the context, and sometimes it's purely the feel of it. You have permission to be intuitive today. You have permission to be "a feather on the breath of God."

THE LONGER WALK

Deeper Dive

This eleventh-century mystic came up with some very forward-thinking images that are both highly visual and penetratingly deep. The terms we use for the lovingly and eternally Divine may or may not be the same as Hildegard of Bingen's, but the underground forks that produce the rivers of commonality feel the same. Try using one of these wise sayings on your next *camino divina* and make it your own.

> O what a miracle to be awake inside your breathing.

> The mystery of God hugs you in its all-encompassing arms.

> Be not lazy in the festive service of God.

> Our souls should be like a transparent crystal through which God can be perceived.

> You're a world—everything is hidden in you.

> The soul is kissed by God in its innermost regions.

"What Is Found": Into Wonder

> I am not alone.
> I straggle.
> I will hold a bowl made of fingers and palms.
> I am hungry for what may be.

> It glows in my hands,
> a yellow dandelion,
> a treasure along the silent path.

> *Descanso*,
> memorial—
> I place my small, yellow contribution
> on top of its cross.

> My empty bowl in front of me again.

> I see a small stick.
> It rests among the branches of my fingers.
> I spy a creek. I throw it in. Where will it go? Where

will I?

I am a part of magnificent Divinity.
I am one of many, one of One.
I am carried by unseen joy.
I am caught up in the circulation.
World-breath. Life-breath.

I am "a feather on the breath of God."

I myself, the begging bowl.
Empty.

Then Filled.

The Scalloped Path

Here are some questions for further exploration with fellow
path-taking pilgrims. After you have experienced the adventure into wonder in your own world, in your own interiors
and intuitions, delve into and dive deeply down into the
exploration together.

1. Where were you in your internal landscape when you
   started out on this *camino divina* walk? You can answer
   this conversationally or choose three to five words that
   express your state or mood.
2. When you read the words "a feather on the breath of
   God," what pictures, if any come to mind? Give any
   details you can.
3. Where did you go on your walk? Did your choice
   have anything to do with this *camino divina* being an
   "adventure into wonder"?
4. What images do the words "feather" and "breath"
   conjure up in your imagination as you reflect on your

journey? Do any other words of Hildegard's have special meaning to you?

5. Did you come across any special creatures, beings, or objects on your path that inspired wonder? Filled your begging bowl? What was it about any one of them that ignited your sense of wonder? Did any become a symbol to you of something wonder-full that you'd like to hold on to as you proceed on your ongoing journey— an eagle, a person, a vista, a cluster of flora or fauna?

6. How do you see yourself as "a feather on the breath of God" in your current circumstances? How have you seen yourself as "a feather on the breath of God" in the past?

Suggested Readings and Other Media

Butcher, Carmen Acevedo. *Hildegard of Bingen: A Spiritual Reader*. Orleans, MA: Paraclete Press, 2007.

The saint is described by this author as an "Über-multitasking Frau." This book is considered Hildegard 101.

Hildegard of Bingen. *A Feather on the Breath of God: Sequences and Hymns by Hildegard of Bingen*. Directed by Christopher Page and performed by Gothic Voices. London: Hyperion, 1983.

Pure and unadorned. A classic.

Hildegard of Bingen. *Vision/The Music of Hildegard von Bingen*. Performed by Emily Van Evera, Sister Germaine Fritz, and Richard Souther. New York: Angel Records, 1994.

Updated versions of Hildegard's musical works; a sort of trans-dance version of the visionary.

Starr, Mirabai. *Hildegard of Bingen: Devotions, Prayers, and Living Wisdom.* Louisville, CO: Sounds True Incorporated, 2008. (Also available on Kindle.)

Introduced along with the author's rich devotional appetizers of thought are Hildegard's words, though the saint's prayers and wisdom are the main meal.

Chapter 3

An Adventure into Amazement

Mary Oliver—Holy Bride Married to Amazement

Mary Oliver would eventually grow up to believe that being within "otherness," those other places that include the beauty of the natural world, "can re-dignify the worst stung heart."[1] She has, indeed, through her poetry, gathered many of the like-minded into her word-lit wake. Her tendency to seek solace in the wild started early in the woods of Ohio, where she grew up. The woods and the words were safe havens for a very difficult childhood.

When she was seventeen, the young writer visited Steepletop, the home of the famed poet Edna St. Vincent Millay. There she became close friends with the poet's proprietor-sister, Norma Millay. Mary Oliver lived there for seven years, helping organize the poet's papers and no doubt continuing to marinate in inspiration within the home of the poet whose writing influenced her own.

She is quoted in an interview with Steven Ratiner as saying:

> My school was the great poets: I read, and I read, and I read. I imitated—shamelessly, fearlessly. I was endlessly discontent. I looked at words and couldn't believe the largess of their sound—the whole sound structure of stops and sibilants, and things which I speak about now with students![2]

And because I, too, am a student in my own school of great poets, she is one I read and read and read.

She is the author of books with names like *American Primitive, House of Light*, and *Blue Pastures*, among many others, and has won not only the Pulitzer Prize but also the National Book Award and a Guggenheim Fellowship.

I remember visiting a friend who asked me, "Do you know Mary Oliver?" This was probably fifteen or twenty years ago. "What does she write?" I responded. "Poetry about animals and plants. She's really wonderful," my friend simply stated. Since then, I've filled out the description my friend offered quite a bit. Mary Oliver writes poetry about poppies and suns and herons and Blackwater Pond and egrets and death and depth and self and mirrors and wonder and mystery, among about a thousand other amazements. She writes about holding in deep gaze the things that stun her with gratitude.

Should I go on? And black oaks and rain and snow geese and morning glories and mindfulness, and ...

Courting the Soul at Shotpouch Creek

"A bride married to amazement."
—"When Death Comes"

The trail near Oregon's Coastal Range is muddy-thick as cake batter. Amid sludge and trudge, it climbs continually upward, a spiral staircase through switchback, switchback, switchback. As a novitiate hiker, my tendency is to keep my nose to the trail, eyes down, watching every slippery step. It is my habit to see beautiful layers of groundcover this way, groundclover, too, and mossy-velvety curly ferns. Today is no different.

On my *camino divina* of the day, I plan to toy with Mary Oliver's immortal line, "I was a bride married to amazement," hoping to savor it, let it rest on my tongue for a while, and melt slowly down into my soul. But as I begin walking, I quickly dismiss this notion. Not the right time, not a true moment. I am a bit anxious today, distracted by the slick of my own path, both physically and metaphysically. My focus is downward, step, focus, step, avoid the snail.

There is something about a true desire, though, that seeks buoyancy—a lifting up to conscious awareness, to the fraternal twin realms of being and doing. This desire doesn't seem to want to sink, to be buried in the mire of danker, heavier worlds. So eventually I can't help myself. I begin the journey. The first word of Mary Oliver's phrase, *I*, starts to subtly move up into my thoughts as I continue to walk thickly on the path, feeling like a stick-in-the-mud.

I—I think, the word itself a stick, standing upright, vertical, not half-horizontal like the somewhat lazy-looking capital letter "L."

I. I stand a bit more erect, myself one of many vertical things currently alive in the forest, a flesh-barked walking tree, perhaps, a moving *I*.

Then the word *was*—the past. *Was*—where *was* I? Was I *present* in the past? Did I have the will? I think about this word, "will." In my own history as a teacher, the posture of the word "will" has become transfigured and defined as "spine," its feeling, its form within my own shape, body, and soul. Strong rod. Uprightness and determination. Fistful of gumption in the gut. Strength. Place of identity, respect, self, and forward movement. "I will."

I feel the rod forming once again in me, starting at my toes, progressing up my thighs, then through the step-ladder of my own spine, up to and through the crown of my head. With neck relifted, positioned now and long out of practice, I hold court in the forest. "Will."

I continue to trudge upward. I grow distracted. It's not always easy to stay with the lessons of poet or forest. My body grows achingly tired. I decide to listen to my own subtleties, the small lessons in my own self, and turn around, gently beginning to descend the tree-lined stairway. As I do, something in me becomes suddenly inspired to look out, across the broad expanse of trees. I remember the long-lost position my neck had regained just moments ago, but once again it falls toward the gravitational pull of the downward view of mud. I hear the rousing choir of wind on pine bough and vow to keep my head erect, my posture straight. I walk carefully now, noticing the ground but not beholden to it. Straight ahead. I let my gaze hold itself elegantly. I am *a bride*.

I look up, the priest is the sky, the clouds are witnesses, white and rolling. A gentle applause of moving streams rushes below. This sleek brown trail is my wedding aisle, my smooth, rolled-out runner. Carefully, I am gliding, pacing, head aloft, taking in a grand audience, letting the world take me in as well, dressed in my own royal gown of humanity.

Just for today, I am queen—of myself. I hold my journal like a holy book; clutched in my hands is the penned-out history and open-paged potential of being "me." The clusters of small white flowers and bell-shaped blooms close to my toes are my bridesmaids. The stately red cedars and Douglas pines in the distance, my groomsmen. I am filled with the grandeur of a vast, air-ribboned, earth-laced ceremony.

Married to amazement. That is what I am. I am now a bride married to this new soul partner of mine, this old friend. This surpriser, encounter-er, paradigm shifter, perspective changer. This spouse embodied in awakening. The veil of recent marvels flows and follows behind. The honeymoon of what's next beckons, "Look up!"

I can almost hear, look all around, eye to eye, soul to soul, clay to clay.

I can *be* as a three-leafed clover, tender and movable, among a green mist of flora, or *be* as the lichen, quiet, still, interdependent with branch and stump; *be* as the moss, soft, present, a blurred gaze to those of us walking by. Or *be* as a presence in the wood and in the world, spine erect, head aloft. *Be* a *bride married to amazement.*

Likely or Unlikely Saint? A Sitting Meditation

> "Someone I loved once gave me a box
> full of darkness. It took me years to
> understand that this, too, was a gift."
> —"The Uses of Sorrow"

When I choose carefully from my own box full of darkness, I don't covet with anxious gaze the darkly dipped nuts, chews, or soft-centers on display. I actually feel as if I *am* the soft-center being selected, chewed up, and swallowed. I choose Mary Oliver as an unlikely saint, not because of her darkness but because of her incandescence. No matter how many murky, mucky trails I walk through in her heavily wooded poetry, I always find luminosity. Something glows from the inside out. Something suddenly shines that before looked rather dull in appearance. "Every morning," she says, "the world is created / Under the orange sticks of the sun." My own ashes seem to come back to life under the subtly blazing "orange sticks" of her words. She is a slow saint. A deliberate saint. A saint who takes the time to watch the change of seasons and to notice more carefully her own. A saint who takes rapture seriously, play seriously, daily immersion seriously.

She wrote a poem once about a she-bear. The poem was called "Happiness." I recall floating upward with the animal as I read it, intoxicated with honey and life, wishing I could be so taken with the gift of the natural world that I, too, could find myself drowning in delight, in seas of honey, in pools of blackberries.

With the box of darkness in mind, as well as the lightness and delight of a she-bear covered in bliss, I imagine that if Mary Oliver were artfully portrayed on a saint's picture-card, she might be holding a thick river of mystery in one hand and a ripe, sweet blackberry in the other, drawing all sorts of humming, buzzing creatures to it. She is held in the thick, sweet slowness of awe and appreciation, unmoved by the temperature of time or the dizzy haze of abacus-counted days.

I love this, and so I say, and so I pray: May I be a saint able to hold deep mysteries, deep rivers—my own box "full of darkness" in one hand, and the buzzing, humming, light of amazing luminous life in the other.

Amen.

Camino Divina Adventure: Into Amazement

Whether you are male or female, think of yourself as a "bride" today. Not in the gendered sense, but in the betrothed sense. Promise. Engagement. Newly married to the potential that awaits in relationship with the day. Today is fresh, different from any other; you walk down the aisle with a new partner named [fill in the day's date].

Your sacred book, your "something borrowed," is Mary Oliver's phrase "a bride married to amazement." Hold it close. Ingest each word, each sound like communion. Delight in each part of the phrase like forkfuls of wedding cake. Be inspired phonetically by what the poet calls "the largess of their sound." Take the time to notice your posture, your gesture, your presence with each step of your walk and each word of her poetry. Then try to notice "something blue" and take it along with you, whether it be sky, or flower, or something deep within your soul. What is blue for you today? What amazes or puzzles you about this blueness? What surprises you about it? What delights you or intrigues you? If the blueness is within, what shade is it? Cobalt or cerulean?

Perhaps, now, try to explore something old. In your new relationship with the day, are you inadvertently taking along with you "old stuff"—attitudes and feelings that linger on from another time, another day? Is there some old business that you might want to take care of first, before you are ready to begin this fresh new relationship with today? If so, what might it be? Can you look at it, and at yourself, with kind eyes, observing it not in judgment, but with curiosity?

Now for something new. How about everything? All that is around you. At this moment. In this place. Remind yourself that you are here. In this new relationship. You are in union with this present moment. And in light of this, are there any vows you'd like to make? To yourself? To the world around you? To Spirit? If so, I encourage you to write them down as a loving promise for the future. Any commitments? Any expressions of gratitude? Any expressions of appreciation? Are there any witnesses around you to notice the festivities of amazement? Any words of wisdom coming to you? And what are the gifts? What do you see on the great gift table of life surrounding you in this moment? What is the reception like today? You are the "bride married to amazement." This is your day.

As you savor your answers to these questions, what internal music and memory-worthy visions float up from the wonder of your own soul?

When you finish pondering these things, I would encourage you to journal about this event. Lay down in delightful legacy the jewels of your own experience. Make this your own meaningful, elegant walk with "amazement." We are all brides, male or female, when we are married to amazement.

THE LONGER WALK

Deeper Dive

Mary Oliver roams through the thin places and the thickets of this world with such elegance, such grace. She doesn't seem to mind dirty hands or muddy feet, and through the muck she finds clarity of mind. Through these experiences, we are treated to her illuminated words. Here are a few more of them to take on your next *camino divina*:

> Your one wild and precious life.
>
> Even to float above this difficult world.
>
> The beautiful crying forth of the ideas of God.
>
> Let the soft animal of your body love what it loves.
>
> Shouting i'm here, i'm here! now, now, now, now, now.
>
> Put your lips to the world and live your life.

"What Is Found": Into Amazement

> Muddy-thick as cake batter,
> a spiral staircase,
> my tendency is nose to the trail,
> slippery step,
> avoid the snail.
>
> I begin the journey,
> fraternal twin realms
> of being and doing,
>
> I hope to
> savor it,

the slick of my own path,
melting slowly into soul.

I—spine,
will, determination.

A bride—the sky,
the clouds, witnesses, white and rolling.

Married—spouse embodied in awakening.

Amazement—veil of marvel flowing, following behind.

The honeymoon of what's next beckons,

I can *be*,
eye to eye,
soul to soul,
clay to clay.

The Scalloped Path

Writer Aldo Leopold calls land "a community" that "yields a cultural harvest...." When I read Mary Oliver's writing, I get that community feeling—brother brown bear, sister black-eyed susan, all a part of the living, supporting, gathering of species. As you gather around the questions below, see yourselves among the broader family of flora and fauna, knowing that in the big picture of things, a cultural harvest may include the coo of a mourning dove or the buzzing wings of a Rufus hummingbird.

1. Do you recall where your "gaze" started out? Across the horizon, straight ahead of you? Looking down at the path beneath or on the shoelaces of your unlaced sneakers? Up toward the future of the day or at the

impending weather presenting itself in the sky? Where do your eyes usually land when you begin something?

2. Did you feel "married" to anything during your *camino divina* experience? United to a place or a moment? Describe if and when you felt in union with the "community" of the land or communing with yourself.

3. Try this little exercise, if you'd like. Play a short "round robin" with your fellow path walkers. In your discussion circle, have someone say the word "bride." Then go around, allowing each of you to say a word or phrase you associate with that word. No extraneous commentary, just a gentle sharing of words and inner worlds. Let this go around the circle a few times. Then try the word "amazement." Then perhaps "married." See what associations are attached to each word and the variety or the synchronicity that appears with them. Talk about these similarities and differences, and perhaps the stories behind the associations.

4. Describe other moments where you experience being "a bride married to amazement" on ordinary days. Share a profound memory from your past where this feeling restored your faith or your sense of well-being in the world.

Suggested Readings

Oliver, Mary. *Long Life: Essays and Other Writings*. Boston: Da Capo Press, 2004. (Also available on Kindle.)

A gorgeous writer is a gorgeous writer is a gorgeous writer, often whether in poetry or prose. Her personal essays here show another facet of this poetic gem of a person.

Oliver, Mary. *New and Selected Poems*, vol. 1. Boston: Beacon Press, 2004.

Between these covers are a few of my personal favorite poems, such as "Wild Geese," "Poppies," and "Morning Poem."

Oliver, Mary. *New and Selected Poems*, vol. 2. Boston: Beacon Press, 2007.

A beautiful collection of poetry that gives the reader, in Mary Oliver's words, a glimpse into "the pinewoods of my inner life."

Oliver, Mary. *A Poetry Handbook: A Prose Guide to Understanding and Writing Poetry*. New York: Mariner Books, 1994.

A slender introduction to the craft by an accomplished writer and teacher.

Chapter 4

An Adventure into the Wild

Clarissa Pinkola Estes—Mother of Perpetual Story

Clarissa Pinkola Estes's own personal tale is woven with many colorful threads, including the blended skeins of her own family heritage. It interlaces the experiences of being born to Mexican immigrants of mixed racial and ethnic ancestry, as well as being raised by people of Hungarian Magyar descent. The deep stories that helped shape her into a virtuosic *cantadora* (storyteller) were told and retold at dinner tables, near laundry baskets, by members of her immigrant family near the shores of the Great Lakes in Indiana.

As a Jungian psychologist, she greatly influenced the growing, fertile field of women's studies. Her work inspired many souls to dive deeply into the mythic fecundity found in the study of the self via the craft of storytelling. A tipping point plunge into this realm by countless people occurred in 1996 when her book *Women Who Run with the Wolves: Myths and Stories of the Wild Woman Archetype* was published, selling millions of copies and sitting on the *New York Times* best-seller list for 145 weeks.

She has said, "The saints had calluses on their hands,"[1] and Dr. Estes is no exception, raising three children as a divorced, single mother, eventually working her way into college graduate status, doctoral work, then practicing psychologist.

When I first met Clarissa Pinkola Estes through her influential writing, I, too, was a single mother, staying up late, getting up early, preparing each day to meet my garden full of childhood faces in the classroom setting, while gently nudging my own two out the front door. A teaching colleague, wise and wolflike in her ways, handed me a book and said, "Here. You should read this." It was *Women Who Run with the Wolves.* "OK, thanks," I replied, shelving it for an unexpected amount of time, not knowing when a 608-page book would fit into my life. When another copy floated my way, I started seeing them everywhere—used bookstores, home libraries, coffeehouses. "I should read this book," I whispered to myself. And I did. Cover to cover. All 608 delectable pages. I don't think it's too much of a stretch to say that it created a seismic shift in me that still reverberates today.

Dr. Estes has said, "Mary is a girl gang leader in heaven." Clarissa Pinkola Estes is a girl gang leader on earth, albeit a saintly one in my book, and I've already got the tattoo.

Braving the Banks of Watab

"Be wild; that is how to clear the river."
—*Women Who Run with the Wolves*

I'm walking the well-ordered campus of St. John's University in Collegeville, Minnesota, gliding past boxes of perfectly manicured flowerbeds. They are neatly arranged by color and texture: "elephant ears" and "fairegardens" nestle up to mauve-colored chrysanthemum bonbons. The trees are all aligned neatly, the lawns frosted with tufts of green, and the streets are clean and tidy. My words for today are *Be wild; that is how to clear the river*. To *be wild* amid the fortifications of a university feels like an oxymoron. Forests of well-bricked buildings stacked in Lego piles seem hardly wild. But the words beckon me, for it is "I" who am asked to be wild, not the environment I find myself in.

Be wild, I hear inside myself. Let go. Let the things around you capture your attention, draw you in. *Be wild*. Let the world take you in this time, instead of you taking in the world.

A tree shivers in a sudden frill of wind. I stop in my tracks. Like a wild cat, my attention is captured by pure movement only. There is a flutter of wings whirring, then gliding, into a branch above; it becomes simply another drape of color on the tree-scape. I am beginning to feel the wildness. I am free from overconsciousness. My reactions are to the actions, not to anything else—like the slide of light on the edges of a field of grass, which appears, golden, then disappears. I am watchful.

I head off campus out to a trail that leads to Stella Maris Chapel, the "Star of the Sea," hoping to continue to remain one with all that's around me. Above me balances a chipmunk. He is munching on a green pinecone, corncob style, with meticulousness and voracity. As he moves, he appears to float atop the lace of branches with so much ease, so much grace. A large gray squirrel then scuttles out of my way on the path. "Oh, don't rush," I say gently. "It's just me."

The sweat on my body oozes out its own delicious answer to the craving for the physical. I walk with steadied pace, then sudden stops. It's about the moment, not the destination. It's about what seizes me there and then, here and now. I let myself be seized over and over again. My intellect drifts away into a sudden sea of non-necessity. No thoughts of "What should I do now?" or "What does this mean?" It's all raw, ruthless surrender to the moment—a hunger for wind on open pores, those microscopic mouths taking in whatever gifts the wild can give.

That is how, continues the phrase. I think about *how*. Hhh. Breath itself. *Ruach*. The word begins with "h." Repeated, it is the sound of panting; I think of animals moving smooth and liquidlike through the forest. Breath. Breath. Breath. Hhh. Hhh. Hhh. Pulse and circulation and breath moving together in a blessed synchronicity. Mmm. To breathe feels good.

How. Hhh, then, "o." Circle of lips. Sign for the endless. Round and round. Circumference of questions within mystery. Eternity in the center of a word. How?

Hhh. O. Whha. The word's own ending, "w," an exhale. And the beginning letter of other words like "why" and "what" and "where." It is a modern rune embedded with digging and desire.

To clear.

The small ponds and marshes I walk by are studded with lily pads and clusters of dead, brown flora. They are so still, so quiet, holding on to their pockets of debris, their deadweight, alongside beautifully anchored yet floating mud-flowers. These wise lotuses hold their own among the decay. But if a hefty wind galloped by or a strong current pulsed forward, there would be a clearance. All weight would be pushed aside, all matter flung away, leaving only movement, water, and the sturdy studs holding heads of flowering beauty. *To clear*. The mind. The heart. The soul. The body. All of these releases are gifts in their own times. All of these, opportunities for freedom and unencumberment, a washing clean to make space for new things, new ideas, new landings on the open surface.

That is how to clear the river.

I arrive at Stella Maris. It is a small and humble chapel, shyly unveiling a flash of blue from its stained-glass windows as I approach. I enter. I ask myself, "What is captured inside these glassy pictures?" Rivers. I find myself enveloped in rivers of glass, flowing all around me, their reflections spilling out all over the floor. Wow. Coincidence?

I am now in the water of it all, swimming in light mixed with indigo, cobalt, and aquamarine, engulfed in pure colored glow. Yet I find the center is completely open, a breath. A place to be. *Be.* Clean. Cleared.

Likely or Unlikely Saint?
A Sitting Meditation

> "I hope you will go out and let stories happen to
> you, and that you will work them, water them
> with your blood and tears and your laughter till
> they bloom, till you yourself burst into bloom."
>
> —*Women Who Run with the Wolves*

When my daughter was transitioning from working at an understaffed homeless shelter on the south side of Chicago—her hair shaved off like Joan of Arc's to "avoid any unnecessary trouble"—to the neat white-sheeted world of twin-sized dorm beds and heady discussions on John Donne and René Descartes at the university, I decided to send her a story. *Gift* her a story. *Threshold* her a story. It was Clarissa Pinkola Estes's mesmerizing reading of "Grandmother Wisdom: The Story of Los Cincos Espiritos" (The Five Women Spirits).

As I tied the recorded story with ribbons of purple, red, and orange, looping each one through its CD center, I wanted this difficult transition she was going through to be laced with wisdom and love. I knew that swirling around that audio-story were a wise godmother, a young fear-filled girl, and some elemental spirit women who juggled fire, wind, earth, and water. I knew that on that CD were words that might stir the flames of my daughter's heart—phrases that rang true to my own experiences, my own core values, phrases like "Women juggle fire so that the fire will not go out." I hoped this gift would be a tonic for her as she moved into and beyond this next threshold experience.

Over the years, stories have become medicine for me. I recall sitting next to a flickering salmon-colored candle, and whispering to my sister, as she awaited major surgery, the tale of "The Little Dawn Boy" as he scales mountains and defies lions, bringing the seeds of beauty and life back to his people. Then again, smoothing my daughter's hair, as she huddled under red rivers of extra-soft blankets, soothing her soul after a major relationship breakup with the story of "The Little Red House with No Windows and No Doors." In that story, the wind urges a little boy further on his journey, the answer to his question somehow held in the palm of his hand.

When I see Clarissa Pinkola Estes as a saint, the "mother of perpetual story," I envision her juggling the powers of the elements in one hand—fluidity of water, grounding growth of earth, change agency of wind, cleansing lick of fire. In the other hand, I imagine dark velvet-voiced words of inflection, reflection, and wisdom, a deep-forked river of story, still and calming. Together, they create a strange and beautiful juxtaposition of upper and lower internal realms.

And so I say, and so I pray: May I allow the sometimes wild elements of life experience to dance wisdom into my soul, while letting the deep river's elements and story bring meaning and richness to them.

Amen.

Camino Divina Adventure: Into the Wild

As you get ready to venture out today, take a few minutes to think about what it means to "be," and to "be wild." Right now, you may be reading this in a living room, at a kitchen table, on your front porch, or somewhere "out there." Wherever you are, wherever you happen to "be," you are part of the landscape, homescape, world-scape around you.

How do you see your "be"-ing in the place where you "be"-gin your journey today? Right here. Before you traverse the broader landscape. How are you currently part of the landscape of living within the very context of where you are? And how does this context—your home, your office, your backyard—reflect your own nature in your natural habitat? Where do you see *you* there?

And what about "wild"? Can you envision yourself as a seamless part of the environment around you, able to observe and be observed? Can you allow yourself to be part of the bigger? Can you be a moving, breathing piece of the verdant and vibrant whole?

It has been a fun exercise for me at times to imagine myself as just one of the other creatures out there delivering themselves into the sequence of the day, trying to get a better understanding of how my presence affects and doesn't affect things, taking time to allow things to affect me. Like weather or sound, trying to be in tune with these things as feathered and furred creatures are. Consider, for example, the amazing hearing ability of owls, with their heads' incredible rotational sound systems. Or swiftlets, famed for their domiciles used in "bird's nest soup"; they use extrasensory echolocation to judge distances in caves. I ask myself, what would it be like if I tuned into just my hearing right now, or my sense of smell, savoring each sound, each scent?

What would it be like for you to do the same? To spend an entire hour purely on sound, the better part of a walk noticing only the scents of things?

On your *camino divina* journey today, be inspired to take everything in with slow sips. Attempt to be nearly invisible, so the world as it usually is can go on with you as intimate guest and as gentle observer. Don your imaginary invisibility cloak and try to become camouflaged within the colors and textures of what's around you.

I recommend taking a nice chunk of time for all of this, if possible. Settle in to being a part of the larger whole. Then, with journal handy, write down what you observe about the environment you have become intentionally a part of, what you sense inside yourself, and anything you notice about how the surroundings experience your presence, or how you blend in seemingly seamlessly and what that feels like.

Allowing the freedom to "be" in the wild and to "be wild" may just help "clear the river" inside. We are all part of the living landscape. We are all part of the ongoing big story of life. "Be wild; that is how to clear the river."

THE LONGER WALK

Deeper Dive

Here are more opportunities to walk out the stories deep inside you and all around you. Clarissa Pinkola Estes's sharp wit and deep waters can be good company to keep when turning the corners in your own life's trajectories or sanding down the edges of the soul. Some of the quotes I've included here are a little bit longer than those in other chapters, so feel free to grab just a phrase or marinate in the whole idea.

> When seeking guidance, don't ever listen to the tiny-hearted. Be kind to them, heap them with blessing, cajole them, but do not follow their advice.

> Tears are a river that takes you somewhere …

> The doors to the world of the wild Self are few but precious. If you have a deep scar, that is a door, if you have an old, old story, that is a door …

… stand up and show your soul. Struggling souls catch light from other souls who are fully lit and willing to show it.

To create, one must be willing to be stone stupid, to sit upon a throne on top of a jackass and spill rubies from one's mouth. Then the river will flow, then we can stand in the stream of it raining down.

"What Is Found": Into the Wild

"Be wild,"
I hear inside myself.
"Be wild."

Pure movement—

a tree shivers,
a flutter of wings,
reaction to action—
golden,
then disappears.

I can merge,
being to being,
stripe to stone,
squirrel to boulder,

craving
moment, not
destination—

what seizes
raw being.

I approach.
Rivers.
Rivers of glass,

light mixed with indigo,
cobalt, aquamarine.

Pure colored glow.

I find the center completely open.
A place to *be*.

Be. Clean.

Cleared.

The Scalloped Path

There's a Native American saying that goes like this: It takes a thousand voices to tell a single story. Word has it that oral storytelling may be as old as human language itself, our ancestors gathering around warm fires, relaying their theories about life and the universe, their experiences—both expected and unexpected—on their daily rounds, sharing their own interpretations of what those experiences mean to them. This is your chance to grasp the nuance of experience around a single place; your chance to gather around the ancestral fire.

1. What did it feel like to be a part of the living landscape? Were there any natural communities you especially felt a part of—the culture of birds, the teeming congregation of insects, the quiet ways of sky and flora? Any others? What part did you play in that gathering?

2. How did you see yourself on your *camino divina*? As wild engager? Quiet observer? Describe the parts of yourself that seemed to come alive while engaged in one of these roles during your walk.

3. If you could weave an impromptu story of your day's adventure, right now, including the interesting details about your own observations, your own ponderings and postulations about the meaning of it all, how would you tell it? What would you include in a five- or ten-minute tale? Give it a try. Share with your listeners your own day's truth-telling.

4. Were you able to be a receiver on the "divine way" today? What was it like to be a participant in the unfolding story of life in the wild?

5. Did any rivers clear for you? If so, what were they, and what was that like? Do you foresee opportunities for further clearing?

Suggested Readings and Other Media

Pinkola Estes, Clarissa. *The Dangerous Old Woman: Myths and Stories of the Wise Woman Archetype.* Louisville, CO: Sounds True Incorporated, 2010.

Includes memorable stories and lessons, including "The Jealous Girls and the Old Woman Under the Lake," "*Las Tres Osas*, the Three Old Re-Weavers of Torn Lives," and "The Ruby Red Fox," stories that stick like healthy, warming porridge in the soul.

Pinkola Estes, Clarissa. *The Late Bloomer: Myths and Stories of the Wise Woman Archetype.* Louisville, CO: Sounds True Incorporated, 2012.

An encouraging recorded collection of truths and tales for the latent bloomer in all of us.

Pinkola Estes, Clarissa. *Warming the Stone Child: Myths & Stories about Abandonment and the Unmothered Child.* Louisville, CO: Sounds True Incorporated, 2006.

A collection of readings given to us by this healer and storyteller.

Pinkola Estes, Clarissa. *Women Who Run with the Wolves: Myths and Stories of the Wild Woman Archetype*. New York: Ballantine Books, 1996.

The book that put Clarissa Pinkola Estes on the *New York Times* best-seller list for a record-setting 145 weeks and captured the feminine psyche.

Chapter 5

An Adventure into the Beautiful

John Muir—Dweller in Forest Cathedrals

In his own words, John Muir describes himself as "poetico-trampo-geologist-botanist and ornithologist-naturalist etc. etc. !!!!" Others would aptly call him conservationist, inventor, activist, wilderness explorer, guide, writer, prophet, citizen of the universe, founder of the Sierra Club, and father of the national parks. But before all those inspired descriptors attached themselves to his name, he was just "John," a small boy born in Dunbar, Scotland, in 1838, a year after Queen Victoria assumed the throne.

At age eleven, his family moved to Fountain Lake Farm in Wisconsin, where later, in his book *The Story of My Boyhood and Youth*, he states:

Nature is streaming into us, wooingly teaching her wonderful glowing lessons, so unlike the dismal grammar ashes and cinders so long thrashed into us. Here without knowing it we were still at school; every wild

lesson a love lesson, not whipped but charmed into us.
Oh, what glorious Wisconsin wilderness![1]

An early word-seeded experience for this lover and protector of the land.

In his ensuing years, his wanderlust in mind and soul took form in the inventing of a study desk with a retrievable book mechanism; discovering the rare orchid, *Calypso borealis*, in the swamps of Canada; and setting out on a thousand-mile walk to the eastern gulf of the United States. And eventually his explorations would take him out to Glacier Bay, Mount Rainier, Yosemite, Sequoia, and the Grand Canyon, among so many others, to be *the* powerful voice in helping to create our national parks system.

He preserved, conserved, reserved, and eventually helped form the Sierra Club "to make the mountains glad."

My first real contact with John Muir occurred in the surreally green woods in Mill Valley that share his name. Otherworldly and alive with lush moss, it felt like the true living-ness of living things outside of buzzing human-inhabited neighborhoods and thrumming, humming streets. Banana slugs, bright as fruit, horsetail ferns, and cool layers of the aforesaid moss decked the old-growth forest with reasons why places like this should be protected. I guess you could say the ghost of John Muir was to be found in the forest's friendly, lush places as a reminder to love the ground under my feet and the flecks of life floating all around me. In his own inspiring words:

When we contemplate the whole globe as one great dewdrop, striped and dotted with continents and islands, flying through space with other stars all singing and shining together as one, the whole universe appears as an infinite storm of beauty.[2]

And besides, who wouldn't love a guy who strings words together like freshwater pearls?

Leafing Through the Layers at Caspers

> "All scars she heals, whether in rocks
> or water or sky or hearts."
> —*John of the Mountains: The Unpublished
> Journals of John Muir*

My old "sit spot"[3] is the place where my friend, a particular timeworn oak, coils its arms outward and upward in a radial growth pattern. Its form turns skyward, its thick-barked waist poised in sun salutation; elegant-aged ballet dancer, frozen in fourth position. This is the same place I once found myself whirling among the crispy crunch of dried oak leaves during a gust of internal freedom. The same place where I spied a spider's half-web of invisible reality, it's magnificent spirals unhinged at two of the corners, appearing to be mysteriously there but not there, causing me to somehow have faith in the unseen once again. The same place where I became an old friend to myself while the oak tree looked on, inexplicably becoming a friend to me as well.

I gingerly fumble my fingers up the bark of this now dear oak, its rough skin familiar, friendly. And as I follow the chunks and chinks in trunk and branch, I notice the stretch marks. Not craggy and painful to look at, but sweetly appearing like baked molasses cookies, soft skin breaking open at some point in its past, now showing traces of movement, places of growth.

"Let it work on you," I can almost hear her say, "the beauty of the scars."

I am thinking about John Muir's words. John Muir's *her*—nature. A devoutly faithful man, immersing himself in mountain cathedrals and praise for the Sculptor of them all, he found *her* out there, too. The lovely salve-bearing, balm-bequeathing *her* who wooed him into the northern California wilderness for years. She, his wooer, his healer.

I say to myself quietly, purposely mixing up the concoction of words: *The beauty of the stars? That's what I know. Glowing balls of light in darkness, pinpricks on a cushion of night. But, no, what about the beauty of the scars?*

I've written jam-red "wound poetry" for years, walking in and out of scar tissue, hoping for redemption through the cleansing regeneration of words, turning bloodstains into blossoms and scabs into smooth paths for new internal trailheads. And I've often forgotten over the years the power of slick-leafed bandages and sunset poultices.

I walk by paddles of beavertail cactus. Their shapes always seem to comfort me in a comical way. They make me think of cartoonish mouse ears made of bright, bobbled, prickly pears—those sticky, painful treats my father used to explode over in happiness, stopping on the side of the road in the searing heat to dare to pick. There was too much joy in their deep dark red, in their spine-guarded fruit, to pass them over. Too much sweetness beneath their scabby skin to fear the painful prick.

I am brought back from red reverie.

Now amid the rich, spiny sculptures here, in the center of Caspers Wilderness Park, branches are sewing the sky together, in crazy-quilt fashion—blue patch, cloud patch. So are the baby squirrels, stitching tree to tree, oak to oak, root to root, loosely, with tiny-footed basting stitches. The whole world feels put back together somehow. Put back. Restored. Amid the prickles. Amid the sores. Amid the broken branches and dying leaves.

"All scars she heals," John Muir said. All scars. I look at the life-worn, human-torn acreage around me. Char scars, growth scars, hack scars. Burns and scorches. Stretches and strains. Axes and hatchets. All scars. In my travels I've seen so many towering tree giants with a black crisping at the center of their hearts, hollowed out by seething forest fire or tinged at the tops by lightning strike. Gored. Gutted.

I have my own white birthing scars, stretch marks, decorating my trunk from life pushing me beyond my skin limit, in the brave pursuit of creating kin, of making someone new. I have a surgery scar, smiling in semicircle, hiding the secrets of a long-ago tumor and it's necessary scalpel slicings—remnants of a time not of birthing but of cutting away, discarding. All scars. Not to mention the monumental ones, hidden in the coils of brain and soul.

She. John Muir's "Nature." That lovely soother and wooer. *She heals.*

In some form or another, *she* has always called me, wooed me, taken me behind bushes, into shadows, revealing something lavish, unearthed: a thistle with hair so brilliant, so purple, it is an anemone of supernova in artichoke form, or a stone so glowingly housed in a watery setting, I mistake it for something otherworldly. She has always lured me with her unusual beauty. But now she heals.

All scars she heals, whether in rocks or water or sky or hearts.

All scars. It's amazing how close the words "scars" and "scares" are. Scars feel like the hardened remnants of past "scares" to me, walking in and out of wounds. Haunted, then eventually coming clean, with a new, slick cover of ground to journey on. And "scar" and "sacred." Too similar in sound too ignore. Scare, scar, sacred. There must be something to this progression.

She heals.

The jam-red of my own heart, brilliant and beautiful as well, rich and pulsing with life, has been wounded so many times. I don't know much about the stories of these rocks, their cracks, their granite edges. Or the dissipating water, its gradual disappearance creating a smattering of weeds in the dry riverbed. Or the sky, serene right now but perhaps holding visions of some past agony, hawks and turkey vultures bearing witness. But I do know my heart. I know its stories well and I know its well of stories. And I know that silt and sky and rough bark of oak tree do something to sand down the raggedness, the ruggedness, those places that catch me every time I get hooked into the pain of my own past. And I know *her*. The soother. The wooer. The healer. And in ways both small and large, in the presence of *she* and *tree,* I feel healed.

Likely or Unlikely Saint?
A Sitting Meditation

"I only went out for a walk and finally
concluded to stay out till sundown, for
going out, I found, was really going in."
—*John of the Mountains: The Unpublished
Journals of John Muir*

I had an old friend who himself appeared to be an extension of the trees. Long, tall, and gangly, with grizzled beard and Ent-like hands, I would not have been surprised if a deep cut in one of his limbs had revealed annual rings. As he talked about "wild nature," his eyes would glow with an innocence that seemed to stretch back to the dawn of time, to the days when the dew glistened on the world like newborn tears of wonder. John Muir seems cut from the same cloth, plucked from the same pool of seedlings, as this wild-eyed, wilderness-wizened friend. The same ken, the same kin. I imagine Muir traipsing through Yosemite Valley like a kid on Christmas morning, thrilling at what the rise of sun would reveal, cherishing the gifts torn open beneath wrappings of shadow and night.

John Muir's enrapture with natural beauty enthralls me. It inspires me to look more deeply when I go out, to find much more when I go in. He is like the ancient hermits, the early Christian monastic desert fathers and mothers, this "dweller of mountain cathedrals," only more evangelical in his approach to preserving the place where "we all dwell in a house of one room—the world with the firmament for its roof ... sailing the celestial spaces...."[4]

When I envision the saint John Muir, I picture a strong, lissome elder adorned with weathered hat atop a crown of unkempt silver hair. Between his fingers there is a wildflower, specific to Yosemite Valley, of course—a Sierra butterweed or a Harlequin lupine. I imagine him taking off his worn-out Homburg and respectfully hanging it up on some granite-hewn hat rack as he enters the invisible doors of creation, into the living room of the Divine, holding delicately the verdant, blossoming decoration he found on the world's front lawn.

And so I say, and so I pray: May I uncover my head, my soul, with awe and wonder in the sacred cathedrals of mountain and desert and sea, beholding the extravagant gifts of beauty blooming at my feet and between my fingers with amazement and gratitude.

Amen.

Camino Divina **Adventure:**
Into the Beautiful

The beautiful book of nature is a wonderful text to "leaf" through. Its pages unfold into so many layers of luminosity and extravagance. The idea of the "book of nature" is said to date back to the Middle Ages, when the world surrounding us—the world above us, and the world beneath us—was considered a valued source of knowledge and understanding, a compendium of wisdom alongside sacred script. Both were looked upon as enlightening and enlivening volumes.

When you go out on your own *camino divina* adventure today, try to keep in mind that you are walking around inside the book of nature, within this illuminated manuscript of natural beauty. Think of this place as a giant three-dimensional forested or river-clad pop-up book, opened up on *this* particular page, on *this* particular day, for you to delight in and discover. This is a prized opportunity to amble about in sacred text. As you take John Muir's words along with you, "All scars she heals, whether in rocks or water or sky or hearts," see if you can decipher where the spirit of these words is engraved in nature, perhaps in places you haven't peered into before. And don't be afraid to speak aloud the questions you have roiling and churning inside you.

As you journey along, consider stopping in front of something that seems to be drawing you in—a weeping willow or a Jeffrey pine, a chunk of granite or a ragged shoreline—and ask quietly, "How do *you* heal all scars?" or "How have *you* weathered battering winds and the erosion of time?" or "How are you continuing to *be healed* through the timeline of stars and scars?" While the tree or rock or shoreline may not speak to you directly, a still, small voice in your soul might, or perhaps a combination of the two: you and the book of nature working together to unlock the mystery of life that is unfolding all around and inside you.

Ask yourself questions as well: What scars are evident, or perhaps not so evident, in the rings and bark patterns of my ongoing growth? Where do I long to be healed? Where have I felt the small but soothing touch of healing in sky, or sand, or beast, or human hand? How did it affect me? How is it still affecting me? How might I open my wounds, my scars, to the touch of nature's healing today? What could that look like? How could I be a partner in that? Am I *the healed* or *the healer*, or both? What do my scars and nature's scars have in common? What kind of beauty might they both hold, either underneath or on the surface?

Walk the questions. Observe the questions. Risk the questions. Write the questions. Seek the answers. In twig, in spine of pine tree, in swath of cloud cover. And then record your impressions. Explore the answers or the hints of answers that may be coming to you in wind or beetle or mossy rock.

Besides the beloved John Muir, another favorite "book of nature" writer of mine is George Washington Carver, "the man who talks with the flowers." He once said:

Anything will give up its secrets if you love it enough. Not only have I found that when I talk to the little flower or to the little peanut they will give up their secrets, but I have found that when I silently commune with people they give up their secrets also—if you love them enough.[5]

That is such a beautiful thought, a wonderful posture to move into. Seek out what secrets the book of nature will share with you today. See what scars she may seek to heal.

THE LONGER WALK

Deeper Dive

John Muir's wanderings went from the volcanic peaks of Mounts Tongariro, Ngauruhoe, and Ruapehu in New Zealand to views from Tiger Hill in the Himalayas, from a "blue forest" of petrified wood in Arizona to the Chattahoochee River country of Georgia. In one of his journals, John Muir writes "… going out, I found, was really going in." It seems as if a foray into nature is really a liaison with the self. Here are a few more options from John Muir to forge new territory in the interiors while making friends with the exteriors.

No synonym for God is so perfect as Beauty.

The power of imagination makes us infinite.

[G]oing to the mountains is going home; that wildness is a necessity.

Between every two pines is a doorway to a new world.

We all travel the Milky Way together, trees and men.

Anyhow we never know where we must go, nor what guides we are to get—people, storms, guardian angels, or sheep.

"What Is Found": Into the Beautiful

Old "sit spot,"
timeworn,
poised in sun salutation,
half-web of invisible reality,
toe-deep in serendipity;

but today is about wounds,
the beauty of the scars,

twinge of pain,
oozing beneath the words.

"Let it work on you,"
I hear her say,
turning bloodstains into blossoms,
scabs into smooth paths from
sunset poultices—
soul aloe.

"Let it work on you."
Red reverie—
blue patch, cloud patch,
amid broken branches and dying leaves.

"All scars she heals …"

cactus flowers with soft-petaled lips
like sudden refreshment,
so supple, a small entryway into healing—

healing cooing,
healing quiet,
wild shooting star flowers,
dove weed,
cottonrose,
wild oats,

the whole world
feels put back together,

somehow.

The Scalloped Path

John Muir hoped "to do some forest good in talking freely around the campfire" with the likes of Teddy Roosevelt. One of many juicy conversations between the president and the prophet-naturalist, I'm sure. While camping near Bridalveil meadow near El Capitan, the "bully" president is quoted as saying, "This has been the grandest day of my life! One I shall long remember!" Whether gathering in a "forest cathedral," beneath a canopy of trees, or under a stuccoed popcorn ceiling, here are a few questions to "talk freely around the campfire" about.

1. What are your best memories of "place," either in childhood or adulthood? What connections did/do you have to the land in those spaces?
2. Were you ever "healed" in some way out in those spaces? How? Does looking back at those times continue to bring some sense of healing? In what way?
3. When you think of nature, do you think of it as *she*, as John Muir does, or in some other way? Explain.

4. Was there a particular vista, creature, or growing thing that specifically drew your attention on your *camino divina* adventure? Did any of them "speak" to you? Did any of them heal you in some way? If so, describe the experience.

5. Did you bring along with you a scar you'd like to talk about? If the scar has a voice, what would it say? If nature has a response, what might it be?

Suggested Readings and Other Media

Dodge, Kathleen. *Day and Section Hikes: John Muir Trail.* Birmingham, AL: Menasha Ridge Press, 2007.

Try a few of these hikes yourself on the famed, aptly named trail.

Fitzpatrick, Jason, director. *Mile, Mile and a Half* (documentary). Warren, NJ: Passion River Films, 2013.

A stunning visual expedition of the John Muir trail, recorded by a team of five artists working in multiple mediums, and friends.

Gisel, Bonnie J., and Stephen Joseph. *Nature's Beloved Son: Rediscovering John Muir's Botanical Legacy.* Berkeley, CA: Heyday Books, 2009.

The beloved botanist at his best.

Highland, Chris. *Meditations of John Muir: Nature's Temple.* Birmingham, AL: Wilderness Press, 2001.

A knapsack-sized book of John Muir's inspirations; great to take anywhere.

Muir, John, and William Cronon. *Nature Writings: The Story of My Boyhood and Youth: My First Summer in the Sierra, the Mountains of California.* Des Moines, IA: Library of America, 1997.

A collection of John Muir's inspiring and rich wilderness writing.

Stetson, Lee. *The Wild Muir: Twenty-Two of John Muir's Greatest Adventures*. San Francisco: Yosemite Conservancy, 2013.

A treetop windstorm, an avalanche ride, exploits on an Alaskan glacier—check out some of John Muir's greatest adventures.

Wolfe, Linnie Marsh. *John of the Mountains: The Unpublished Journals of John Muir*. Madison, WI: University of Wisconsin Press, 1979.

A peek inside John Muir's richly descriptive journals dating from 1867 to 1911.

Chapter 6

An Adventure into the Heart of Things

Rainer Maria Rilke—Saint of Centers

Rainer Maria Rilke entered this world, and Prague in particular, as René Karl Wilhelm Johann Josef Maria Rilke, a name that would later be altered to the aforementioned "Rainer" when a lover recommended he try on something more "masculine." This theme of transfiguration began early, his mother dressing him in "beautiful long dresses" as a child, potentially trying to recover her lost girl, a baby daughter who died when the infant was only a week old. Ralph Freedman, in his book, *Life of a Poet: Rainer Maria Rilke*, says that "until the end, the poet knew that real life finally exists only within, waiting to become something other than itself."[1]

Born to German parents and raised in Austria-Hungary in the last quarter of the nineteenth century, Rilke found himself in military school, then later boot camp to prepare for service in World War I, an excruciatingly uncomfortable set of occupational and educational clothing that never fit around the contours of his fragile physical health and deep poetic sensibilities. He did, however, connect over time with brilliant thinkers like Leo Tolstoy and Auguste Rodin. Serving as the sculptor's secretary influenced and transformed Rilke's work as a poet. His own poetic influence on the world places him high in the ranks of best-selling mystic writers like Rumi and Khalil Gibran. His life, though, ended at age fifty-one, his grave marked in epitaph with his own unfolding, petaled words:

> rose, o pure contradiction, desire
> to be no one's sleep beneath so many lids.

I, too, was drawn to his mystical words, believing he was a female poet, contributing to the confusion regarding Rilke's gender identity. I guess, like many, the "Maria" pulled me into the identification vortex, despite his choosing of the "masculine" Rainer name. Regardless of whether he was male or female, I found Rilke's center and I was drawn in because he helped *me* find *mine*. His words, "Center of all centers, core of cores, almond self-enclosed and growing sweet—all this universe, to the furthest stars and beyond them,"[2] gave me comfort in my own expanding universe, where heart and soul at times felt uncomfortably flung into the farthest galaxies.

I needed my saint of centers, I still do, and was glad that among life's unpredictable unfoldings I found him.

Nearing the Sea of Rolling Gold at Santa Ysabel

"Do the heart-work on the images
imprisoned within you."
—"Wendung" (Turning-Point)

I choose the Santa Ysabel trail—just outside the apple-pie town of Julian, California, swarming with tourists—because I know out there in "the beyond" I will feel space. I also know that I will have to walk my personal altar, my soul-stuffed self, filled with ego trinkets, faded-out experiences, and pseudo-sanctified indulgences into this broad open landscape. I will bring *me* with *me* wherever I go, for better or for worse.

I look forward to the vastness, a swath of blue sky over a sea of rolling gold. And I look forward to the sparseness—a contrast to the dense, lush forests of Washington State where I live—just dotted here and there with the presence of gnarled oaks, hearty, dusty, and green, and some tall chunks of granite appearing out of nowhere like the heads of Easter Island. I look forward to the breath that the landscape creates, spaces between objects. Islands of metaphor amid seas of serenity.

With Rilke in my mind, and his poetic phrase in my hand, "Do the heart-work on the images imprisoned within you," I immediately ask, "Where is my heart?" It immediately answers, "In a tired place." An interior image begins to emerge—this picture of a gangly, dangly, Mexican-style milagro heart, with beautiful twines of aortic valves falling outward in blue and red, shadowed by hints of black. These words are emblazoned on it like a banner, DEEP TIRED. At the heart of my flesh-adorned altar, the heart speaks its truth. I try to listen to its voice. It seems to long to radiate those familiar orange and golden spindles found on the simple, holy art of tin and resin—flames, pulsing with energy and light, the symbol of the "sacred heart." But in its current state, it does not. My heart is not popping out of my chest with power and wonder but works where it always lives, locked inside my rib cage, doing what it always does, pumping out its life-juice, quietly, deeply.

On today's trek, echoing Rilke's words, I know my heart-work is before me. How do I care for this deeply symbolic organ? I wish I could cushion it, set it on a velvet pillow and let it rest for a while. It always does so much for me.

I emerge from my altar of the interiors to this shrine of the world: Santa Ysabel Open Space Preserve Trail. This sanctuary is now paler green than when I first started on the walk, though not very long ago, highlighted with a layer of gold among the blowing oats. Cows appear as moving stones.

I gaze back into the cavity of my own heart-space. What more can I ask of this tired organ? This muscle that takes on troubles with sincerity and holds them like a doting mother. What can I *do*? What can I *undo*?

How can the effort of creating an interior resting place become more effortless?

And what is my *heart-work*? What is my heart trying to say to me in the wilds of Julian?

As I walk, images are all around me: round-barreled bodies of cows, rust red, black midnight velvet, smoke-ghost white. There are gem-quality bluebirds, sapphires, peeling themselves from the sky and landing on earth. Wild oats, miraculously lit up from within, their hulls highlighting the horizon. A lone tree. Gatherings of granite. I ask myself, "What is my image in their eyes? If they could speak, how would they describe me as I walk along? Droopy girl? Tired slump? Little swamp lantern lit up from within?"

What are the *images imprisoned within me*? I don't know yet. A tired heart milagro? A flutter of sapphire wings moving freely out from the bars of rib cage? How am I imprisoned in images of myself? I hear the black shadow hovering behind aortic valves, telling me over and over how flawed I am. This voice hinders me from using my wings. *How can I break free?*

I listen to my tired heart again. "Rest. That's how you break free. Rest from words. Rest from work. Rest from worth. Lay down your head on the pillow of beloved-ness, no matter who you are, where you are, why you are; being a part of the landscape of glowing oats and bejeweled birds is enough. Being a part of this holy shrine of beauty and belonging is more than enough."

I take it in. I let these wise whispers do their work. I don't know how, but my heart feels rejuvenated. Rested. *I* feel rejuvenated. Rested. The pillow of belonging, of beloved-ness, has done its work. *This* is the image imprisoned within me. *This* is my illuminated landscape.

I have done my heart-work.

Likely or Unlikely Saint?
A Sitting Meditation

"I am circling around God, around the
ancient tower, and I have been circling for
a thousand years, and I still don't know if I
am a falcon, or a storm, or a great song."

—*The Book of Hours*

At poignant points in my life, I could describe my internal state as the "almond self-enclosed," a phrase taken from Rilke's poem, "Buddha in Glory," because of the almond's hardness as well as its beautiful creamy-white center. Bittersweet. Literally. A source of nourishment and a pit, both in its physical and metaphoric forms. Sister to the stone of a peach, brother to the seed of an apricot, the almond is both nut and center, "center of all centers, core of cores," the bowel of the fruit. I could relate to that in both pain and glory.

Rilke may not have meant to refer to the almond as anything but "sweet," but in his words I somehow feel the complexity of the thing, a centrifugal force of meaning in its hardness and its softness, and in its family ties to the bitter inedible, the pit, its life-giving cousin.

Circles. Pit. Flesh. Skin. Air … Circles. Seed. Sweetness. Color. Life … Circles. Stone. Fruit. Forging. Fortitude. Spirals that move outward from the heart of the fruit, "to the furthest stars all beyond them."

I choose Rainer Maria Rilke as a likely or unlikely saint because of his centers and his spirals, his veering toward the inward and his movement toward the outward. I choose him because he is someone who can live within the mystery, circling around the "ancient tower" of the Divine, and not know if he is "a falcon, or a storm, or a great song." And yet he is a ponderer, who goes out "to the furthest stars" and "all beyond them" to experience "your flesh, your fruit," the sweetness, the pith of the Divine.

He inspires me. That word "inspires," so close to images of the spires—the pinnacles of cathedrals, soaring upward to that airy place of falcon, storm, or song. So close to images of the "spirals" found all around us, the flight patterns of red-tailed hawks, curling, unfolding fiddlehead ferns, elegantly golden ratioed nautilus seashells.

I imagine Rainer Maria Rilke, saint of centers, holding in one hand an almond—substantive; central to hull, and fruit, and tree; representative of both the bitter and the sweet—and in the other a spiral, be it seashell or galaxy or fiddlehead fern, coiling outward into larger and larger spheres of hope and mystery.

And so I say, and so I pray: May I hold deeply my "almond self-enclosed" center with reverence, love, and presence in one hand, while allowing the spirals of beauty and bewilderment to unweave, uncurl, and unfold freely and fernlike in the other.

Amen.

Camino Divina Adventure: Into the Heart of Things

Where is your heart today? As a spiritual director, I often look for that moment when words drop from head to heart. When communication takes the "down" elevator to gut. When thought stops floating out into the atmosphere after demanding our constant attention and feeling raises its hand, words finally lodging themselves into the heartfelt truth of the matter. Today, on your *camino divina* adventure, take your heart along with you. I mean, really. Tell your head you really appreciate it and all the cognitive spinning and whirring it does, but it's the heart's turn for an outing.

As you venture onto whatever physical path you choose, try stopping a few or many times along the way and listen carefully to what your heart is saying. Sometimes people see "the heart" as a combination of inner mind and intuitively mined emotion. The word *lev* in Hebrew means "heart," but with more to it than you think. Jeff A. Benner, founder of the Ancient Hebrew Research Center, writes on the center's website, "To the ancient Hebrews the heart was the mind, the thoughts…. The first picture in this Hebrew word is a shepherd staff and represents authority as the shepherd has authority over his flock. The second letter is the picture of the floor plan of the nomadic tent and represents the idea of being inside as the family resides within the tent. When combined they mean 'the authority within.'"[3] As you walk and pause along the way, try to heed your *lev*, your heart's "authority within," with sensitivity and respect.

And don't be discouraged—"courage," by the way, means "to stand by your heart." It can take patience and time to discover that deep listening place. Perhaps ask yourself questions like these: Where am I emotionally right now? (No judgments, please.) What is my heart-work? How can I gently honor this physical and metaphorical organ, this place inside me that houses so many important things? How is the landscape, the views outside me, working on the inside of me right now? What kind, helpful words would I tell myself if I could? Say them to yourself, in an audible whisper or on the page. How would that answer take shape if it were portrayed in an image, a picture? Give it a try, sketch it out, and see what it would look like.

Here are other questions that might peel themselves open on your journey: What images are imprisoned inside you? Are they positive, negative, or both? Can you set them free? Can you create a new image portraying them being set free? What would that image look like? Describe it in words, draw it in pen or pencil, or use natural objects around you to make a montage in sticks, stones, shells, or pine branches. Can you imagine enjoying the possibilities of their freedom?

Remember the pillow of beloved-ness and belonging I referred to earlier? Be sure you take advantage of its presence on your trail. Rest frequently. Enjoy acceptance as you never have before. Heart-work can be both exhausting and rewarding, both buried treasure and dirty fingernails. "Do the heart-work on the images imprisoned within you" and then invite your head back into the picture to congratulate you on the hard work you've done.

THE LONGER WALK

Deeper Dive

The "saint of centers" knows the edges as well. He walks the rim of the canyon as well as the interiors of the canyon floor. Here are a few more poignant phrases to work with if you choose to take more walks with Rilke:

> The Earth is like a child that knows poems by heart.
>
> Live the questions now …
>
> The only journey is the one within.
>
> The purpose of life is to be defeated by greater and greater things.
>
> We see the brightness of a new page where everything yet can happen.
>
> [D]rive the last sweetness into the heavenly wine.

"What Is Found": Into the Heart of Things

The beyond.
Space.

Personal altar, soul-stuffed;
I will bring me with me,
wherever I go.

Where is my heart?

Mexican-milagro,
aortic valves falling outward in blue and red,
beautiful twines,

on it, a banner,
DEEP TIRED.

Tin and resin flames,
holy art,
"the sacred heart,"

my heart-work is before me.

A flutter of sapphire wings,

"rest from worth";

wild oats, miraculously lit up
from within,

"lay your head on the pillow of
beloved-ness."

No matter who you are,
being this holy shrine
is more than enough.

Rejuvenated, rested.
Illuminated landscape.

I have done my heart-work.

The Scalloped Path

Back in Rainer Maria Rilke's day, salons were inspired gatherings propagated, in Horace's words, "to please or educate" one another. They lived out their heyday during the "age of conversion" in the eighteenth and nineteenth centuries, but continue on as opportunities for an exchange of ideas. Whether or not you choose a salonnière to lead your collection of shared experiences is up to you, but here are a few questions to get you started:

1. Did you discover any images "imprisoned within you"? If so, what were a couple of them? Which was the most poignant? Why? How did you discover it?

2. Was there a point on your journey where you noticed that your head-work dropped down the elevator into heart-work? What did you notice about that? Was there a different quality to the sound of your own intuitive voice? The heart voice versus the head voice?

3. Did you do any other valuable heart-work on your *camino divina* adventure? If you feel like sharing, use pictures or metaphors to describe the work you did or are doing.

4. How did the exterior landscape of your walk work on your interior heart-scape or soul-scape this time around? What living things around you created some form of friction in working the inner spaces?

5. Did you take the opportunity to rest into beloved-ness or acceptance? What tensions surfaced? What moments of respite? How can either one of these help you do the heart-work you may want to do?

Suggested Readings

Baer, Ulrich. Translated by Andrew Hamilton. *The Rilke Alphabet*. Bronx, NY: Fordham University Press, 2014.

Twenty-six essays focusing on twenty-six words that shed light on the intriguing thought-life of the poet.

Barrows, Anita, and Joanna Macy. *A Year with Rilke: Daily Readings from the Best of Rainer Maria Rilke*. New York: HarperOne, 2009.

Taste a bit of Rilke every day of the year, through the words of his poetry, prose, letters, and journals.

Freedman, Ralph. *Life of a Poet: Rainer Maria Rilke*. Evanston, IL: Northwestern University Press, 1998.

Ralph Freedman, a professor emeritus at Princeton, shares his thoughtful examination of the poet in eloquent prose.

Rilke, Rainer Maria. Translated by Stephen Mitchell. *Duino Elegies and Sonnets to Orpheus*. London: Vintage International, 2009.

Perhaps Rilke's two most venerated poetry sequences, masterfully translated.

Rilke, Rainer Maria. Translated by Stephen Mitchell. *Letters to a Young Poet*. New York: Merchant Books, 2012.

Rilke's letters to one of the many young poets who wrote to him, including some sensitive and sage advice, as well as a window into Rilke's own life.

Chapter 7

An Adventure into the Present

T.S. Eliot—Prophet of the Eternal Present

Thomas Stearns Eliot was born a Brahmin. Yes, a *Brahmin*. In the Boston sense. This term, referring to the traditional Indian caste system, was given by Oliver Wendell Holmes to a class of New England gentry whose roots within their family trees separated and sailed to the New World's shores in the early waves of settlement. They are often associated with the erudite and a Hahvid (Harvard) accent, as well as seeing their own destiny as guiding lights to the American experiment. T.S. Eliot was born *into* Boston Brahmin as family culture but was birthed near the shores of the Mississippi River in St. Louis, Missouri.

"Tom" as he was known as a child, suffered early from a double hernia, keeping him tucked away from the usual recreations of childhood. Because of this, he found himself immersed in the physicality of books like Mark Twain's *Tom Sawyer* and other wildly adventurous volumes. It was said by his friend and biographer

Robert Sencourt that Tom "would often curl up in the window-seat behind an enormous book, setting the drug of dreams against the pain of living."[1]

Writing under the influence of Edward Fitzgerald's *The Rubaiyat of Omar Khayyam*, T.S. Eliot wrote his first poem at the age of fourteen. He went on as an adult to write such notable poetic masterpieces as "The Waste Land," "The Four Quartets," "Ash Wednesday," "The Hollow Men," and the well-known "Love Song of J. Alfred Prufrock." In 1948 he was the recipient of the Nobel Prize for Literature. And though born an American, he ventured back to the land of his pre-1669 ancestors, becoming a British citizen and finishing out his days there, being buried in East Coker, where a plaque near his ashes reads: "In my beginning is my end.... In my end is my beginning."

I was in college, sitting with a cluster of students around a large, laminated-wood conference table, when I first discovered that I may "have measured out my life with coffee spoons," drawing the quote from T.S. Eliot's "Love Song of J. Alfred Prufrock." We were studying Eliot's poetry with a very Thomas Stearns–passionate English professor. The poet's lines were so striking, so able to cut between "soul and spirit," "joint and marrow," that I felt that Something Larger was Speaking to Me. And it made me teeter on the thought, balancing on the back side of a spoon, "Do I dare Disturb the universe?" In absentia, Professor Eliot was beginning his work on me. I then fumbled my way through sticky, thorny labyrinths of uncharted life territory in my twenties and thirties, discovering that, in Eliot's words from his poem "Little Gidding," often we can only "be redeemed from fire by fire." Church Warden Eliot was prodding me into the smelter of the real. And now, I forever come back to the words "to arrive where we started and know the place for the first time," as Mentor Eliot's wisdom from "The Waste Land" continues to echo back into the continuum of who I am and who I am becoming. I am grateful his words consistently bring me back into the labyrinth of the eternal present.

Living Within the Labyrinth at Chinook

"To arrive where we started and know
the place for the first time."
—"Little Gidding"

I approach this labyrinth on Chinook land, like so many others, with relish, anticipation, and perhaps a little anxiety. I like the idea of a labyrinth—lots of curves contained in a small space, usually placed in an intriguing outdoor setting, with the walker able to see the whole thing in one visual panorama; the layout of all the coming convolutions from a view above. It gives me the feeling of a topographical experience of life in miniature.

Flashback to my first labyrinth in Santa Fe, New Mexico. Oh, the excitement I felt at spotting it from a distance: *It's here. I'm here!* With great abandon, I entered the red clay spiral, hoping I would come out a little bit different at the other end, which was actually the same end. And I did. I felt refreshed. I felt as if in metaphor I had given my upcoming life path a small exploratory test run in that little walking space. Anticipation. Entrance. Experience. Centeredness. Rest. Emergence. Gratitude. Whew, it felt good! And so did the other labyrinth experiences I have had: engraved in the floor at Grace Cathedral in San Francisco, carved into a red dust heart shape at Ghost Ranch in northern New Mexico, crafted out of bungee cords at Camp Asbury in New York.

At the entrance of this one I feel the same, mostly. The stones are carefully placed to corral and guide my feet snugly toward the center. There are talking alder trees all around me, creaking and swaying as they tend to do, almost eerily voicelike. I have scrawled on a piece of paper T.S. Eliot's words from his poem "Little Gidding"—"to arrive where we started and know the place for the first time"—and that's where the tinge of anxiety comes in. I've walked the labyrinth of my own life for many years now. Where will it take me this time as I arrive again "and know the place for the first time"? What will be revealed in this small adventure? As I come again to this stopping point, will the mental measuring stick show me as more wise and wonderful than before, or stunted—the growth mark on the living room wall penciled with signs of stasis or even shrinkage. I don't know. I walk on.

The curls of the labyrinth, like those of life, are always unknown. Because we get the squealing treat of believing we see the whole thing at once, we think we know it, but we really don't. Every time I enter a labyrinth, I always *always* forget where the circuits will take me. Even if it's the same kind of labyrinth I've walked before or in the very same location. I *always* forget the pattern. If I'm in a buoyant mood, this can be a delightful process, imagining that I'm going to the left but actually going to the right. Believing that I'm near the center, but twisting outward toward the farthest curve of the path. Thinking I'm done, when I'm only halfway there. It can feel surprising and exhilarating. When my soul is flagging, however, I feel frustrated. *Haven't I figured this out yet? How many times have I walked this? I should know this!* Hence, my life in miniature.

I come back to the now. I realize that the beauty of the thing is that I'm actually *doing* it, not just *observing* it. I have not chosen to merely look at pictures of the eleven-circuit Chartres Cathedral style or the classic seven-circuit labyrinth, but am actually trying it out, walking it out, working it out, once again. As I've always done. *Doing it* puts me in contact with the real. As I walk past chunky rocks embedded in the dirt and surrounded by sprigs of grass and wildflowers, I am suddenly taken back to a moment in childhood. It is a place with a funny name, "Santa's Village" in southern California. There in the woods of the San Bernardino mountains I felt the same connection as I do here—part of the natural world. Little feet, little steps. Arriving once again, and "knowing the place for the first time."

I'm also reminded of a time when I was at Orama with a small learning community in New Zealand. A group of students marked their days studying abroad by placing a stone and a token of memory in a spiraling path to record in miniature the indelibility of their experiences there. Now these stones here, on Chinook land, are doing the same for me, creating touchstones of memory on the arrival points of my life. *Who was I back then at the labyrinth in Santa Fe? At the one at Ghost Ranch? At the one at Camp Asbury?* I can answer that. Excited and young, and in a swirl of turmoil. Then a little older, more contemplative, tiptoeing through the mud of my past decisions. And once again older still, wiser still, forging through the unknown circuits, but happy with the floating flower I was becoming. Same me but arriving again, "knowing the place for the first time"; knowing the space called *me* better and better, as if for the first time.

And here I am again. With the chance to experience *me* once again, but as *me now*. With many markers left behind, like white stones in a Hansel and Gretel forest, hoping to find my way home. I come to the center of the labyrinth. There are tokens everywhere. A beautiful, interiorly smooth oyster shell. A broken piece of crimson glass. A large chunk of sparkling purple amethyst creating diamonds of light. A bracelet engraved with "shalom, paz, he ping, peace, mir, salaam, paix, shanti, frieden …" A safety pin. An orange and black tiger-striped rock I left here a month ago. I'm not sure why, but sitting here in the middle of it all I'm feeling akin to rocks and wind. Maybe it's because I, like they, also inhabit earth and air, the seen and the unseen.

Though T.S. Eliot's phrase still continues to linger in my mind, another wisdom teacher steps forth from the shadows. "Be here now," Ram Dass says. I need that reminder. I'm tempted, as many of us are, to leave behind the present moment to record some future memory: a picture on a smartphone, a potential entry in a blog, or a post on Facebook. Always tempted to report back rather than report here.

In this spirit, I can almost hear my internal wisdom speaking to me: *Gina, let the dragonfly enchant you for a while. Spy out the dandelion lighting up with the sun at the far side of the labyrinth. Appreciate the warm stones held under the cup of your palm. Already there. Trust yourself.*

Those last words are a breath of fresh freedom. I always forget that these two words—trust yourself—are often the ticket to my own internal liberation. Wow. I really can. I've put in the work. I've walked life's long labyrinth for a while now. And is there really any other way to *be* in the present moment other than by truly trusting oneself? The word "confidence" comes from the Latin *confidere*, or "having full trust." When I feel confident, I'm trusting myself in the moment. I can feel that now. I know that doesn't imply that everything always works out as planned or that I won't encounter potholes to trip over on my own pathways toward knowledge. But I am confident. I can step off the labyrinth into the labyrinth, the treasured symbol of the place that starts where it ends and ends where it starts into the larger winding wilderness of wildflower paths and unexpected life turns. It will all unfold as it unfolds. I can confidently reenter the eternal present. But this gift I can always give as I do: to trust myself.

Likely or Unlikely Saint?
A Sitting Meditation

> "What we call the beginning is often the end.
> And to make an end is to make a beginning.
> The end is where we start from."
> —"Little Gidding"

All time seems to be compressed in the poetry of T.S. Eliot. If there ever was a fleshing out of the scientific theory of time-space compression—a phenomenon that alters the relationship between those two—within the universe of words, it would probably be spoken in the eloquent vernacular of Thomas Stearns Eliot. His thoughts can be mind-bending. Spirit-altering. Soul-stretching. I sometimes find I enter one of his poems as if rocketing into a black hole, but suddenly come out the other end into a blossoming opalescent supernova. His images are incredible but, like all great panoramas, they should be taken in slowly, eyes digesting the vision with great appreciation and rumination.

The eternal present this prophet offers us isn't the eternal stagnant. It's the wrapping around of experience, the full circle, that brings us to the same place but not the same internal space and not quite the same iteration of who we were before. I see the *eternal present* as being surrounded by a room of wisdom mirrors. It's not like a carnival fun house, where you see new distortions of yourself at every turn. But more like a series of soul-sensitive reflective x-ray machines where you can see the layers of who you are and who you've been in ever clearer, ever more radiant images. In the spirit of carnival talk, the fair may be the same but the quality of the fare is different. What you bring is served up more nuanced, even improved each time you come back, though in the same place and to the same mirror.

When I imagine this prophet of the eternal present, this likely or unlikely saint, I see T.S. Eliot poised in the center of a labyrinth, that stopping place of eternal stillness, allowing the windings and bendings in life's convolutions to just be. He sees them but is not moved by them ... yet. They are coming, they are going. The river of experience will surely be entered once again, but stopping at the threshold of the eternal present lets you be and lets you see. It is within that deep place where you can observe the moment and preserve the moment, noticing the timelessness of it, the holiness of it. In his hand is a token—it could be anything, a feather, a note, a stone—that honors through symbol this moment. He places it on the altar of the present. It marks time so we, visitors of our own pasts, can muse with consideration and appreciation on the forward moving time line.

I want this, too, and so I pray, and so I say: May I stand in the stillness at the center of my own life's labyrinth, holding the tokens of each moment as testament to who I am and who I've become.

Amen.

Camino Divina Adventure: Into the Present

There are labyrinths everywhere. Not always the rock-edged Celtic or stone-laden cathedral styles, but crafted into cityscapes as well. I'm thinking of the Plus 15 elevated walkway system in Calgary, Alberta, or the Minneapolis Skyway System in Minnesota, as examples. They may not follow the nature-hewn convolutions of circuited flow toward a contemplative center, but they are definitely walking paths that with intention could lead to an internal center. There tokens of thought, memory, and imagination are left by city-dwellers who imbue those labyrinths with personal meaning.

As you begin your *camino divina* adventure today, think about place. Where could you go to "arrive" where you "started and know the place for the first time," either symbolically or historically? Since the labyrinth is an archetype of walking life out while going within, is there a place in your city, in your neighborhood, or in your local park system that creates a sense of guided meandering, whether by tunnel or by crafted path? An arboretum? A skyway? A walkway? An actual labyrinth at a local church, synagogue, museum, or cathedral? Or is there a place you would like to go back to, a landmark in your own personal history where you can arrive where you started? You can take the time here to check in and discover what subtle changes or major transformations have occurred throughout the years.

Once you've chosen your place and are ready to step into the entrance point of this moment, take a few seconds and make sure you are truly present. Here. Now. Fully open to this precious time. And trust yourself. Be your own best companion as you walk. As you begin your trek, allow noticings and nuances to knock on the doors of your conscious thoughts. And be respectful, not judgmental, of what floats in.

What connecting points are coming into view as you encounter a crossroads or a twist on the path? Is a memory triggered? What pictures from the past remind you of who you were and who you are now on your own life's trajectory? As you walk, how does the physical winding of the path you're moving on right now reflect the twists and turns of your own personal passages? What are the twists and turns occurring in your life right now? Do they mirror any windings from the past? Do you radiate an inner smile of joy or triumph knowing you got through those? Are there any lessons from the past you can bring into the present?

When you reach a "center," a stopping point on your *camino divina*, what does it feel like to be at rest? Do you allow yourself breathing space to just be? Try to sit in that still point, that center, for at least a few minutes, if not longer. This is a great chance to check in and see if you're able to really rest well for a time. If not, ask yourself why not.

If you could, what tokens from memory would you set down at the center to remember who you were last year? Five years ago? Ten years ago? Twenty years ago? As you are right now? If you'd like, write down what they might be, sketch a picture of them, or create a montage to take with you. How would each token honor the person you were at each point on your journey, even though now, in hindsight, you may see your flaws? Then, picking up those tokens and holding them in your mind's eye, how will you proceed, carrying your past along with you lovingly, carefully, and moving on? How will you finish out your walk today as you acknowledge yourself at each stage of your life while also being fully present to who you are now?

As you finish your walk "out of the center," whether physically or internally, or both, notice what feelings and thoughts glide through and perhaps even guide you the rest of the way. How did you arrive where you started today "and know the place for the first time" or know yourself for the first time?

THE LONGER WALK

Deeper Dive

An initial reading of T.S. Eliot's potent and poignant lines of poetry becomes a dive into the deep end of the wisdom pool. Swimming around in them for a while makes the experience of the water even sweeter. I recommend several dips into his words, perhaps even a few *camino divina* walks contemplating the same line but experiencing it in different places to see if the words and meaning penetrate your soul even further each time.

> Only those who will risk going too far can possibly find out how far one can go.

> Love is most nearly itself / When here and now cease to matter.

> Teach us to care and not to care.

> You are the music / While the music lasts.

> Only by acceptance of the past, can you alter it.

"What Is Found": Into the Present

> Labyrinth,
> curves contained
> in one visual panaroma,
> life in miniature.

> Engraved in the floor,
> carved into red dust heart,
> crafted out of bungee cords,

> stones corral and guide my feet,
> a small exploratory test run
> in a little walking space,

> "to arrive where we started and know the place for the first time."

> The curls of the labyrinth,
> are always unknown,

left, but right,
near center, but twisting outward,
done, when only halfway there.

I come back to the now—
chunky rocks,
sprigs, wildflowers,
little feet, little steps,

arriving once again, and "knowing the place for the
first time."

A broken piece of crimson glass.
Purple amethyst creating diamonds of light.
A safety pin.
Same me,
hoping to find my way home.

And here I am again.

"Already there. Trust yourself."

Fresh freedom.
Ticket to internal liberation.
I can step off the labyrinth into the labyrinth.

It will all unfold.

The Scalloped Path

A colloquy is simply a conversation, almost literally a collecting of *loqui*, or talk. As you gather to digest the twists and turns of the internal and external walk of life, symbolized in miniature by the labyrinth, remember that some also see it as walking the petals of a large rosette, moving toward a center of stillness and wholeness. At your gathering, or colloquy, enjoy how the petals unfold within as you come together, sharing your own collections of words, completely present to the present.

1. What was your "labyrinth" and where did it take you today? Was there a center? A beginning and an end? If so, what did you discover there?

2. Were there places you felt you "arrived" once again, getting to glimpse the many versions of you that brought you to the place you are now? Which versions of you did you reflect on? Could you appreciate them for what they were? For who you are now? If so, share these reflections and appreciations.

3. Were you able to trust yourself? If so, what changes, if any, did you notice in your ability to relax, sense some internal freedom, inhabit who you are more?

4. The labyrinth has been referred to as a self-alignment tool. Are there places within you that feel more aligned now? If so, what are they and how do they feel more in line? Or are there places that are at least stirring and seeking alignment? If so, where are they?

5. If you could place tokens or symbols at the center of your self today, after your *camino divina* experience, what would they be? What would they represent? What would they honor?

Suggested Readings

Crawford, Robert. *Young Eliot: From St. Louis to The Waste Land.* New York: Farrar, Straus and Giroux, 2015.

Drawing extensively on Eliot's personal papers, this biography takes the reader into the unfoldings of an eventually renowned poet.

Eliot, T.S. *Old Possum's Book of Practical Cats*. New York: Mariner Books, 1968.

A delightful romp created for Eliot's godchildren and friends that eventually inspired the Broadway production of *Cats*.

Eliot, T.S. *T.S. Eliot: Collected Poems, 1909–1962 (The Centenary Edition)*. New York: Harcourt Brace Jovanovich, 1991.

Included in this collection are the poet's most notable works, including "The Four Quartets," "Ash Wednesday," "The Waste Land," "The Hollow Men," "Gerontion," and "The Love Song of J. Alfred Prufrock."

Worthen, John. *T.S. Eliot: A Short Biography*. London: Haus Publishing, 2011.

A dip into the controversies surrounding the man and a view of his life in retrospect.

Chapter 8

An Adventure into Darkness

John O'Donohue—Friend of Thresholds

Raised in a limestone valley in the Burren region of Ireland, where the unique land formations look "as if they were all laid down by some wild surrealistic kind of deity,"[1] John O'Donohue always seemed to be most comfortable in the "thin places," those veil-thin openings into the spiritual world. He was born in 1956, and the landscape of his own life experience brought him from romping the karst valleys of Connemara with his "mystically sacred" stonemason father to becoming a novitiate priest in north County Kildare, and then to Tübingen, Germany, as a doctoral student, mining the rich terrains of Hegelian philosophy and Eckhartian theology. From his dissertation, he is credited with developing a new concept of Person that was cited by the highly respected journal *Review of Metaphysics*.

With the publication of his book *Anam Cara: A Book of Celtic Wisdom* in 1998, his own sage collection of words became a startling success to an academic and priest who enjoyed living out much of his life in solitude. Over time, he eventually became a spiritual word-minstrel of sorts, finding himself speaking at such diverse places as the University of Oxford and the Greenbelt Festival about issues touching on our deep yearning to belong, "the duty of privilege is absolute integrity," and the importance of beauty and how it differs from glamour.

I was caught off guard when I stumbled onto, then tumbled into, his words while looking up wise passages by wise people on the Internet. I was compiling a personal collection of daily meditations to share with my mentally mobile, rampantly questioning teenage children. In a "Celtic Wisdom" folder I created and printed, John O'Donohue's name kept showing up over and over … and over. *Who is this guy?* I quickly ordered *Anam Cara* and feasted gleefully and gluttonously on his words for days. Then, meal finished, I ordered a second helping, *Beauty: The Invisible Embrace*, gorging on that spiritual wisdom faster than I could digest it. Afterward, I started ruminating and then ingesting his insights at a sensible pace, taking notes, grazing, and engaging the same wise helpings over again for a more satisfying, spiritually nourishing experience.

I've gone back to the writings of John O'Donohue so many times in my life that he's literally become a spiritual habit. His wisdom, insight, and penchant for poignant blessings have become my life event *go to* in so many ways.

He crossed the other threshold at age fifty-three, through that thin space that leads out to the other side. The world misses him terribly, and, needless to say, so do I.

Meandering the Interiors of Midnight at Double Bluff

"Darkness is the ancient womb."

—*Anam Cara: A Book of Celtic Wisdom*

Double Bluff Beach. Someone told me there would be inescapable moonlight there, so I went. I imagined it radiating off all the liquid surfaces, creating some sort of beacon so I could see in the dark. Driving toward the water, the first two lights I view in the road are about wheel-high, reflections off the eyes of an adolescent coyote, one of my animal totems, zigging and zagging the street's broken yellow line, no doubt frightened by the big red monster we call the family truck. He is my harbinger. My nightlight. Young, off-kilter, confused by strangers. I am feeling a bit nervous, too. Pawing my way through the darkness is not my first impulse, although I've done it before, on several occasions.

In this context of darkness, I can't help but think back to my kidney surgery a couple of years ago. The time spent under the knife went fine; the recovery, though, was thick and dank and difficult. Falling in and out of consciousness, confused, searching for my light saber, my light savior, but not finding it, or It. Pawing once again.

Darkness is the ancient womb. I know this ambiguous walk isn't necessarily going to be easy, though if I were to choose a companion of words, John O'Donohue is a good one. Yet, truly, I am excited, too. This is a chance to redeem that other moment *obscura*—to seek some illumination on the purpose and presence of dark places. I remind myself of another set of wise words, this time spoken by nineteenth-century poet Sarah Williams in her poem "The Old Astronomer": "Though my soul may set in darkness it will rise in perfect light; I have loved the stars too fondly to be fearful of the night."

There are black holes in this sand. Chances to trip. And their little caverns of shadow punctuate a moonscape. I don't know if this comforts me or disturbs me. So many nicks and pockmarks in the "ancient womb." So many dips into potential missteps. I carefully pad my way through, combing the shore on tiptoe, then look up to see the massive scattered bones, white and luminous under the steady eye of the moon. They are blockades of bleached driftwood, but look more like some great archaeological dig, some grand unearthed graveyard for dinosaurs or whales looming in the night.

I think back again to that time of darkness I couldn't explain myself out from. "Where were you?" not knowing which "you" in particular I am referring to. The big You. The little you. The mutual (Y)you. It was a hard time back then. A lonely time. I'd love to unravel that emotional skein, find out where everybody was.

Darkness is the ancient womb. I repeat this to myself like a mantra. Comforting. *That sounds so nurturing.* Mothering. A place somehow I'd like to be born from. Maybe I can be born from it tonight. Maybe I'm always born from it.

Though I'm not feeling very Pollyanna, I notice little silver linings everywhere—the edges of the shore, the trim of the ocean's nightdress. Silver. Silver. It's my friend the moon again, throwing her illuminations out recklessly. Mirrors all over the place. Shattered light, scattering itself into glowing shards, shaking with the wind and water. Like neon. So crazy bright. *Man,* I think, *I wish the moon was there that night.*

Then my eyes graze the ground and land on the sandscape around my own feet. Footprints in all directions. Human. Dog. One I don't recognize—flat, round, and even, with little pearl-shaped toes, almost a perfect bear paw. No bears on Whidbey Island, though. Did a child make this? An adult? Could this be a carefully carved-out petroglyph from the day's artful revels? Looking at the wild variety of imprints, what it shows me is that we have all been down here. At one time or other. In the ancient womb.

Double Bluff Beach is a unique place in that the large driftwood bones are stacked all over the sand landscape to make shelters for humankind, or any kind. They look like ancient wooden tents, sukkahs, tiny hermitages. I crawl into one. Another womb of sorts. A womb within a womb. It feels good. The moonlight sneaks in, too. I feel as if I have company. I suppose some may wonder if it's a true darkness experience if the sky is fat full of moon. I suppose, though, no matter what, the eyes always adjust, no matter how slight or bright the increments of light.

I'm finding I like the womb. Especially the womb within the womb. I feel cared for by hands I don't know on a beach where others have traveled. Someone has crafted this retreat I now sit within amid the Tenebrae. *Darkness is the ancient womb.* Somehow, she is the Mother of us all, this dark place. And this place, with its bleached tree bones, almost feels like a rib cage. And I, the pumping heart. I went to a *hangi* once, a traditional Maori gathering meal in New Zealand, where the master of the house explained to me and my comrades that when you enter a Maori home, you are entering a mother. The walls, her skin; the wooden beams, her rib cage. I have never forgotten that. I can once again see the sacredness of it.

I eventually crawl out. One must be birthed sometime. When all is ripe.

I realize again it's always a risk to come out. There are comforts in the known. Even if the comforts are more familiar than friendly. And there are risks inherent in the "out there." Even if the unseen outcomes are good. I see Moonfriend still hovering above, a witness to tonight's journey. I notice, though, that the waters have calmed, the wind has died down, and the moon herself, for the most part, appears whole in the water. No longer scattered in fragments along the surface. I have been hoping for this moment, even though the broken light was magnificent. I want to see the luminous orb in its altogether-ness. Yes, there is a "glass darkly" sense here, too, in that the image in the looking glass doesn't remain perfect at all times—disturbed by a subtle breeze, a gentle wave. But finally, her reflection is whole, and I am witness.

I look up, double vision. Whole moon above, whole moon below. Twins. One appearing in detail in water, as real as the other in sky. And I guess they both are real. Whether made of basalt, anorthosites, and breccia or made of glass and tears, reflection and rainwater. They are in actuality just one. Together. Image and creator of image.

I wonder, too, about my own reflection if suddenly kindled in the darkness.

Shining. Silver. Shattered. But also whole.

Likely or Unlikely Saint?
A Sitting Meditation

"Your soul knows the geography of your destiny."
—*Anam Cara: A Book of Celtic Wisdom*

If someone were to hand me a love note to give to my soul, it might well begin with John O'Donohue's words from *Anam Cara*: "Your soul knows the geography of your destiny. Your soul alone has the map of your future, therefore you can trust this indirect, oblique side of yourself. If you do, it will take you where you need to go, but more important it will teach you a kindness of rhythm in your journey."[2] When I began reading his works, I felt like I was opening up love notes all day long. I was running full tilt to the post office box of my heart, cramming my tiny silver key into its lock, opening its contents, and drinking in the soul-soothing melt of his words like an ardent secret admirer. Yes, he was *that* good.

I often go back to our *anam cara*, our soul friendship, via the treasured texts he's left behind. I'm sure many others are also rummaging through their beloved boxes and books of his love letters, breathing a deep sigh when they've read one of his nourishing lines once again. In Gaelic, *anam cara* means "soul friend" or "soul mate." Our saint, John O'Donohue, continues to explain that, "in this relationship, you are understood as you are, without mask or pretension. When you are understood, you are at home."[3]

When I think of John O'Donohue, this likely or unlikely saint, this Friend of Thresholds, I picture a heart of clay, a piece of truly human interior, once tucked into the darkness of my own body, gently held in both hands, and a lorica, or breastplate, of blessings fitted over the body and soul, protecting the beloved from the potential harm lurking in the darkness of the unknown, the *anam cara* protecting the beloved from the unkind lashings of the ego and the world.

I want this, too, and so I pray, and so I say: May I hold my own clay heart with gentleness and kindness, and cover myself with the lorica of love.

Amen.

Camino Divina Adventure: Into Darkness

A journey into "the ancient womb" takes some preparation. The interior and exterior prep work done for this *camino divina* experience may be very helpful, and make for a more vibrant exploration. To start, think ahead to a place or places where you will feel safe and not overly distracted by the unnerving unexpected (cars, other walkers, and the like). I would even recommend a quiet escort if you have one, someone who may possibly be doing his or her own *camino divina* work as well. It is important to find a place where you are safe enough from distractions so that your soul and heart can roam free. I chose a beach. A backyard can actually work quite well. A womb can be carved out in many spaces. Once you've found a safe environment, spend some quiet moments preparing the interior regions. Give your whole being a break. Take several minutes or more to enjoy the still spaces around you. Be like a child floating in amniotic fluid and let go of anything else besides breathing and being.

When you are ready, walk or stay sitting. The choices of these moments are yours to settle into. Feel the quality of the dark. Take the time to feel it. If you were to put words to being present to this night's darkness, this early morning's darkness, what would they be? What old words or ideas seem to attach themselves to the word "darkness" for you? For me, they can be words like "oblivion," "blindness," "a void," "ignorance." As they come up, try to shelve them, if you can. Imagine in your mind's eye a set of shelves and place those old images and ideas attached to darkness, each one on its own shelf, just for now. When you've done your initial darkness clearinghouse work, take a few moments' rest in between, then try to experientially gather some new feelings, new words and images about the word "darkness" as they come to you. Be as open as you can. What are other qualities of darkness? Look for subtleties.

What do you notice in the dark? Have things shifted or become clearer to you as the time unfolds and your eyes adjust to what is? Are there physical adjustments you need to make when moving, like proceeding more slowly, more deliberately, more thoughtfully? What is it like for you to slow down? Think about this. What qualities emerge in you, in your thought-life, in your soul-life, when you slow down? John O'Donohue uses the expression "slow time" in his piece "A Blessing for One Who Is Exhausted." He talks about the joy that "dwells far within" slow time. I have grown to love slow time. I have grown to practice slow time whenever I can. Try to "dwell far within" slow time yourself right now.

After you've given yourself some time in the darkness, how can darkness as "the ancient womb" nourish and nurture you at this time? What is sustaining you in this place? Are you finding shadows of rest? Nooks and corners of release? Are there any thoughts, past or present, seeking incubation? Gestation? Take some moments to contemplate these questions, and see if some answers begin peeking their heads out from the darkness.

As long as you feel comfortable, take your time in the womb of darkness. For many of us, it is a rare occurrence to have ample time with the companion of night. See what it can teach you, what you may be teaching yourself.

THE LONGER WALK

Deeper Dive

We can be an *anam cara*, a soul friend, to ourselves as well. The dramatic and challenging landscapes of our interiors can be sharpened or smoothed by the experiences we draw alongside of them. Another walk with the words of the poetic and prophetic bard John O'Donohue can continue to hone those places into our best selves—the selves of belonging.

> I would love to live like a river flows, carried by the surprise of its own unfolding.
>
> May the relief of laughter rinse through your soul.
>
> We need to remain in rhythm with our inner clay voice and longing.
>
> Behind your image, below your words, above your thoughts, the silence of another world waits.

Grace is the permanent climate of divine kindness …

Take time to see the quiet miracles that seek no attention.

"What Is Found": Into Darkness

Inescapable moonlight,
on liquid surfaces—
some sort of beacon;

searching for my light saber,
pawing once again.

Black holes in the sand,
a sea of unknowns,

so many nicks in "the ancient womb"—
a place I'd like to be born from.

Footprints.

A carefully carved petroglyph.
We have all been down here.

I now sit amid the Tenebrae,
a womb within a womb;

a shelter, a sukkah, a tiny hermitage,
the walls, her skin; the wooden beams, her rib cage.

"Darkness is the ancient womb."

When all is ripe,
I eventually crawl out.

One must be birthed sometime.

The Scalloped Path

In ancient Ireland, the Seanchai (pronounced Shan-na-kee) collected the stories and tales from alongside the unfolding history of the clan in order to preserve the epic narrative of their people. They held the gift of the gilded tongue and continued to retell the tales trippingly. Whether you have a natural knack for fluidity of narration or just a desire to recount your tale, a Gaelic proverb tells us that "two shorten the road." Telling our stories to one another not only helps forge wise pearls from experiential oysters, but it also creates worthy companionship. Here's a chance to tell your story.

1. Recount your adventure into darkness in the form of a great unfolding story. What emotions, like reticence, uncertainty, or epiphany, played a part? How are those woven into the story?

2. Did you have a companion on the journey? Whether it be human, hound, or silvery orb, what part did it play in your comfort, distraction, or illumination? Were there places where a "bard of gratitude"—a recounter of those epic moments—might be in order, reciting those things that brought joy or assistance?

3. Did any revelations emerge? If so, what were they? Did they surprise you? Startle you? Were they about darkness? Illumination? Birthing? Incubating?

4. Did any metaphors emerge from the experience? Darkness was like ____ to me, now darkness has become _____ to me. The "ancient womb" was a _____. If so, share them.

5. John O'Donohue was a master at creating places to "bless the space between us." In the spirit of two shortening a road, consider creating a collective blessing by having each person in your group write a line or two that begins with the phrase "May you …" Think about how you want to bless one another as you emerge from "the ancient womb" and share it as an offering to each other. As John O'Donohue says, to give a blessing makes a person or an object a "live sanctuary" … "benevolently permeated by the breath of blessing."[4]

Suggested Readings

O'Donohue, John. *Anam Cara: A Book of Celtic Wisdom*. New York: Harper Perennial, 1998.

A beloved best seller on both sides of the pond.

O'Donohue, John. *Beauty: The Invisible Embrace*. New York: Harper Perennial, 2005.

A reminder that we live for more transcendent things than what can be consumed, and, as Fyodor Dostoyevsky said, "Perhaps it is beauty that will save us in the end."

O'Donohue, John. *Eternal Echoes: Celtic Reflections on Our Yearning to Belong*. New York: Harper Perennial, 2000.

Potently and elegantly addresses our desire for "being and longing."

O'Donohue, John. *To Bless the Space Between Us: A Book of Blessings*. New York: Doubleday, 2008.

My go-to book for poetically crafted words of blessing for nearly every occasion.

Chapter 9
An Adventure into Unseen Worlds

Joy Harjo—Sister of the Eyes That Can Never Close

In her memoir, *Crazy Brave*, Joy Harjo states, "A story matrix connects all of us. There are rules, processes, and circles of responsibility in this world. And the story begins exactly where it is supposed to begin. We cannot skip any part."[1] In the spirit of those sage words her own story unfolds. It begins as a braiding together of two tribal strands: the Mvskoke (Creek) and the Cherokee from the lands we call Oklahoma, Alabama, and Georgia through the bloodlines of her mother, Wynema, and her father, Allen.

These familial weavings within her childhood created the difficult combination of the "water spirit" of her father and the "fire spirit" of her mother. Anger and alcoholism were at times the painful result of "people of water" who, as she states in her memoir, "will always search for a vision that cannot be found on earth...."[2] And fire people? They "can consume and be consumed by their own desires." Living within the cauldron of this toxic mixture, compounded by an abusive stepfather, propelled the young artist to concoct a recipe for her own dreams far, far away in the state of New Mexico.

First, Joy Harjo was accepted into the Institute of American Indian Arts in Santa Fe for talent as a visual artist. Then her deep love and penchant for music and poetry blossomed into her creative life as well. She eventually birthed such books as *Maps to the Next World: Poems and Tales* and *The Woman Who Fell from the Sky: Poems*, as well as several solo albums and the acclaimed *Letter from the End of the Twentieth Century* with her band, Poetic Justice.

And there is much, much more to the story. But the place where hers intersects with mine is somewhere on my life's journey when I read the line: "... I wished to make a map for / those who would climb through the hole in the sky," and I found myself scrambling up the rungs of the wind to try to get there. I guess "gawking" or "standing agape" or "grappling" for the hidden worlds she reveals in her poetry might be accurate ways I can verbally describe the intense satisfaction and desire created by lapping up the fresh springwater of her words. It is a spiritual event to sit in the grottoes of her poetry—a flower-and-charm–bedecked mystery, a dream catcher of a moment, and yet somehow warmly familiar.

Just like the mystical nature of her poetry, I can't quite remember when I first encountered her work, only that it showed up one day. Her name and the nature of her voice reverberated in my mind, and I followed the trail like a lost child in the woods, recognizing the glowing stone markers of her words: "We are in a dynamic story field, a field of dreaming. Move as if all things are possible."[3]

Unearthing the Unknown along the Hood Canal

"I know I walk in and out of several worlds each day."
—*Winged Words: American Indian Writers Speak*

I've heard about so many unseen worlds. Good people have told me about the secret doings of elementals, those living greening spirits that tenderly nurture each gentle shoot of grass and massage the soil under every growing plant. For them, it is a rich world of quiet beings tending to the souls of waterways and the communal lives of forests. Others have told me about the presence of ancestors, their giant souls moving in migration from forgotten place to remembered existence, sometimes poignantly extending aid or a timely word as quiet and brilliant as the sun, as mysterious as the wind. I think about the unseen worlds I've encountered on this earth, either directly or inadvertently. Growing up, I was often reminded of "the great cloud of witnesses" who have gone before me, those heavenly cheerleaders who urge us onward from beyond wisps of horsetail clouds. And the angelic realms—places from which benevolent and powerful protectors representing stalwart values like truth or courage or love—watch over the ripening earth with hope and expectancy.

Nearly every night I enter the unseen world of dreamtime, where parts of myself are transformed and transfigured somewhere within my own great unknown. This is a shape-shifting world. I've been a wingless flyer, grazing the tops of lapis-roofed cathedrals or shearing across the tumbles of pebbles on a somewhere shore. I've been a young African American girl, all pink checks and braids on a dusty Southern road, and a Native American apprentice, nuzzled by my animal totem, the deer, and plunging below the surface of the water toward the Great Turtle, where, I've read in some native lore, we all learn to live and breathe.

As I walk through today's hidden doorways, I try to notice a bit more. I put on my soulful infrared glasses and see what I don't usually see.

The first world I notice is the seasonal world. There are hints of a sea change here. Trees that just last week were verdant and lusty with summer are now beginning to flaunt fringes of yellow, just a few, just on the edges. The sunlight, so loud and glorious, has turned a tinge toward subtlety, humility, peaceful resolution. I can almost sense a changing of the guard—summer's lively sprites making their exodus southward, while autumn's caretakers paint the world in golds and plums, building a quiet bridge into winter. Seamless poetry.

I make my way to the tidelands along the Hood Canal on the Olympic Peninsula and gaze at world number two. A great serpent is flicking its cloud-tongue in a world of air. An air stream ripples through mackerel sky, invading its presence, breaking apart its ethereal scales and transforming it into some new cerulean picture. The sky world … wind is creating blustery stories among the animal kingdom that will make for a good chirp or twitter of whimsy around the nest or burrow tonight. Who knows? They may become good yarns in the ongoing history of migration tales told by Canadian geese, recalling that wild day of wandering along the Puget Sound.

Below me I see world number three. Shore world. Sand world. Oyster world. Their exoskeletons crunch like broken dishes underfoot. Some ovals are still whole, facing upward, their silky undergarments of opalescent white displaying the pure clean fabric of interiors often hidden behind crusty shells. What is the color of my bones when illuminated with light and soul? What mother-of-pearl brightness colors flesh and bone when lit up by the animation of spirit? Some oysters flipped downside up display beautifully frilled skirts. How in the world do creatures create such delicate furls from earthly minerals and crustacean instinct? Nearby is a purplish pink blush on a clam. Same question, different process. How? What marvelous brushes create a sunset on a shell from the inside out?

Water mixes with wind and makes perfect liquid scales that would be the envy of any mermaid slipping by. I then look up to floating wings in "W" formation and the dark curves of windy feathers and wonder about the secret lives of seagulls, the hidden homes of vultures. Yet another world. *I know I walk in and out of several worlds each day*. I've run into so many today and yet with time and commitment I can discover so many more: clusters of barnacle communities on rough red rocks; red ice plant fingers pointing outward as they show up on the gathering of groundcover; yellow daisylike flowers emerging from the marshes while their purple cousins blossom near a raccoon's secret shell collection stash. And these are merely salty tideland stories. I haven't even begun to touch the hidden harbors of my own personal unseen worlds this day. What actions can I conjugate from the dreams of my own mind, my own making? Where do the intentional drifts of thoughts and prayers go? Who hears them and what is their translation when entering the music of the spheres? Can I learn to listen for the answers as they come? Can I trust that, in some form or another, they will?

White birch branch is unclothing her thick white bark, once again revealing the story of the seasons. Alder leaves above me are chewed into green lace by a micro-world that ticks on and on, whether my sight and soul acknowledge it or not.

I know I walk in and out of several worlds each day.

The question is, will I try to take notice of them, observe them, even enter into them for just a brief span of time to mine the riches of their parallel and integral universes? Can I trust them as I walk over their thresholds and through the doors sprung open to me? In these places, am I able to seek out teachers who may hold wisdom rich and different than my own? Like a good student, can I take it in and, if it resonates, make it my own?

The tale of the tideland skies now turns stormy. It has become a solemn gray veil for the tired afternoon sun. This world is folding in for now and I will need to seek out another one, a dry one perhaps, over another threshold … into another world.

Likely or Unlikely Saint?
A Sitting Meditation

"You're coming with me, poor thing. You don't know how to listen. You don't know how to speak. You don't know how to sing. I will teach you. I followed poetry."

—*Crazy Brave: A Memoir*

The Woman Who Fell from the Sky, a book of poetry by Joy Harjo, fell into my lap several years ago. The cover was a brilliant blue concoction of starry sky mixed with earthly symbolism. It felt as if the sky had fallen onto the woman, me. As I pored over the poetry, there was little if no distance between the rungs of the upper realms and the lower ones, the divine ones and the earthly ones. Jacob's ladder, once scaled by heavenly beings, was now completely accessible to us clay-born types. As I read more, personal journeys and histories peeled themselves off the wafer-thin pages of ancient books and poised themselves as perennially present in the here and now. I liked the collision of these seemingly disparate worlds or, better yet, the seamlessness of these worlds, held together within the leaves of this book.

Deep down inside, I think I've always truly craved seamlessness—the fabric of existence wreathing through its many universes with the soothing texture of silk and the tried-and-true toughness of hemp. Harmony and Unity leading the way. I am me and you are me and we are we … well, you get the picture. All the worlds, seen and unseen, making sense together. A healthy, ever-lasting, universal body of worthwhile meaning.

Joy Harjo, likely or unlikely saint—sister of the eyes that can never close—feels like a seam-binder to me; a closer of gaps. Perhaps it's because her ever-open viewing portal can somehow see the continuity of all things. Her words create a coupling between worlds. No compartmentalization. No distinct division between physical and spiritual. No perimeters surrounding the pretend borders of future or present or past. When I imagine this saint emerging from the cradles of the Creek and Cherokee nations, I see a woman whose hair is a sea of sky, dripping with the jewels of stars. In her hands she holds a ladder where all the clans—wind and water, the visible and the invisible, east and west, the fleshed out and the thinly veiled—travel seamlessly between worlds, travel uninterrupted within the One World where all of these exist.

I want this and so I say, and so I pray: May I carry with confidence the sea of unknowing sprinkled with the stars and inklings of knowing while allowing the ladder that connects all of my worlds to hold space for me where I can walk freely in joyful pilgrimage.

Amen.

Camino Divina Adventure: Into Unseen Worlds

Each day we are surrounded by layers and layers of hidden worlds, from the meticulous workings of microbiology to the secret weavings of mind and soul; from the secluded living spaces of the animal world to the mystical possibilities of angel and ancestor. Whether any of these are actually hidden or just unnoticed often depends on the focus of the eyes and the intention of the heart. As you set out today with the phrase "I know I walk in and out of several worlds each day" in your hand or in your mind, choose a few worlds you would like to explore.

One may be "all things hidden in shadow" and might include those living things that make domiciles out of the sunless places. This might also entail an exploration of your own shadow side or parts of you that are usually cloistered from the light of your usual consciousness.

Another could be "sky land." Instead of looking down or straight ahead, spend some time scouting out the world above—the patterns of clouds, the winged population, and anyone or anything you imagine dwells there. Spirit? Begin a communication with Spirit. Ancestor? Speak to him or her in that realm. Angel or celestial Being? Start the conversation. You may get to know better one or all of whom you seek, or even yourself. One of my spiritual directors once encouraged me to create a written dialogue between myself and God. Literally, on the page, I wrote, *Gina*: and then a thought or question following my name. Then *God*: and then a thought or answer following. I gleaned so much wisdom in doing this. Of course, this takes time and a commitment to listening deeply and lovingly, but it was and continues to be an amazing practice.

Another possibility might be all the secret wonder that's held within a ten-foot circumference. You might be surprised how much is actually there. I tried out an exercise once created by philosopher Rudolf Steiner. I was to choose an ordinary plant that I came across in my daily rounds and do my best to sketch its appearance over and over each day for a week. Each time I drew it, I got to know that plant better and better—its tiny details, its hidden worlds. I would recommend trying this or doing the same daily kind of noticing but with the "sketching" of words to describe what you see, all the nuances and metaphors.

You can also make a list of other hidden worlds you would like to look into, including engaging the fascinating underworld of water or nooks and crannies in the city. I had a friend once who decided to follow a pattern of walking three blocks, then turning left, over and over for a day, to discover what hidden worlds show up in the city. He said the results were fascinating. Maybe you want to explore the internal spaces of unlocked creativity—what inspiring art form, science form, or word form have you been itching to try? Now is your chance to do so under the auspices of "exploring hidden territory."

Whichever unseen layer you pick, give yourself some time in it. And go back again! The discoveries you make during your exploration may be the trail to untapped wisdom you will find within yourself and your world.

THE LONGER WALK

Deeper Dive

The many worlds available to us may be hidden, but they are often explorable. Sometimes the further in you venture, the more flits of meaning begin to appear and the little footlights start to flutter illumination onto your path. Take the time to try out one or a few of these provocative thoughts from poet Joy Harjo and see where they take you.

> A story matrix connects all of us.
>
> I can hear the sizzle of newborn stars, and know anything of meaning, of the fierce magic emerging here.
>
> I am witness to flexible eternity.
>
> All acts of kindness are lights in the war for justice.
>
> [W]e exist together in a sacred field of meaning.
>
> I am not afraid of love or its consequence of light.

"What Is Found": Into Unseen Worlds

So many unseen worlds—
greening spirits massaging
soil under every growing plant,
giant souls moving in migration,
mysterious as the wind.

Dreamtime,
a shape-shifting world,
where we all learn to breathe
below the surface of the water.

Within today's hidden doorways,
there are hints of sea change—
summer's sprites making their exodus southward,
autumn's caretakers painting the world in golds and
plums.
Seamless poetry.

Sky world,
a great serpent is flicking its cloud-tongue
in a world of air, breaking apart ethereal scales,
morphing some new cerulean picture.

Shore world,
exoskeletons crunch like broken dishes underfoot,
their silky undergarments displaying the pure clean
interiors
hidden behind crusty shells.

What is the color of my bones?
What mother-of-pearl brightness
colors these scaffolds of flesh and bone?

White birch branch unclothes her thick white bark,
revealing the story of seasons.

Alder leaves are chewed into green lace
by a micro-world that ticks on and on.

"I know I walk in and out of several worlds each day."

The Scalloped Path

The word "pau-wau" or "pow wow" originally comes from the Narragansett tribal word meaning "magician" or "he dreams." This term with its Algonquin roots refers to a gathering of shamans or spiritual leaders. The get-together eventually became a celebration of unity, a chance to connect communities. As you come together, unified in your desire to appreciate the unseen worlds all around you, celebrate by unveiling with rich words the discoveries you've made, the layers you've uncovered, the realms of existence you didn't know were there.

1. Share a "hidden" world you explored more deeply on your *camino divina* adventure. Where was it? What did you discover there? What more did you find out about it than you already knew? Was it the world you intended to explore or did it unfold before you in an unexpected way?

2. Did you run into any other layers or realms of existence that you hadn't intended to? Within yourself? Outside of yourself? What were they?

3. What were two or three favorite details you discovered on this journey? A texture? Some sort of small visual feast? A dialogue with the unseen? An integration of plant or animal communities you have never seen before? Something else? Put those details into words.

4. What will the deeper knowledge of an unseen world you discovered bring to your everyday life? What will this awareness give to you?

5. What other hidden worlds would you like to explore in the future?

Suggested Readings and Other Media

Harjo, Joy. *Conflict Resolution for Holy Beings: Poems*. New York: W.W. Norton & Company, 2015.

Her most recent collection, as poignant as ever.

Harjo, Joy. *Crazy Brave: A Memoir*. New York: W.W. Norton & Company, 2013.

An eye-opening, poetically, and delectably written autobiography—a generous slice of the poet's life.

Harjo, Joy. *Letters from the End of the 20th Century*. Albuquerque, NM: Mekko Productions, Inc., 1997.

Described as a classic contemporary native recording, it lifts Harjo's poetry off the page and floats it into the realms of voice and music.

Harjo, Joy. *Winding Through the Milky Way*. Santa Fe, NM: Fast Horse Recordings, 2008.

Poet and musician combine in this audio recording juxtaposed between earth and sky.

Harjo, Joy. *The Woman Who Fell from the Sky: Poems*. New York: W.W. Norton & Company, 1996.

A dreamy collection of poetry that embodies her idea that "the leap between the sacred and profane is as thin as fishing line."

Chapter 10

An Adventure into the Surprising

Flannery O'Conner—Our Lady of the Christ-Haunted

Flannery O'Connor describes herself as a "pigeon-toed child with a receding chin and a you-leave-me-alone-or-I'll-bite-you complex."[1] She was born in the year 1925 in Savannah, Georgia, and made her debut on the world scene at age six, when the British newsreel production company Pathé News filmed and distributed the young O'Connor with her trained backward-walking chicken. She states, "I was just there to assist the chicken but it was the high point in my life. Everything since has been an anticlimax."[2]

At age fifteen, she was devastated when her father succumbed to lupus, a disease that would eventually take her life as well. Post–high school, she would go on to college, studying the social sciences. With a scholarship to study postgraduate journalism, she decided to pursue a master's in creative writing instead. Under the literary influences of people like William Faulkner, Pierre Teilhard de Chardin, Fyodor Dostoyevsky, and

Simone Weil, she went on to write short stories and eventually two novels. This was a task not so extraordinary for a gifted writer, but to have the words "grotesque" and "violent" waft in the wake of her publication credits were, for a staunch Catholic writer, unusual. In her own words:

> I am always having it pointed out to me that life in Georgia is not at all the way I picture it, that escaped criminals do not roam the roads exterminating families, nor Bible salesmen prowl about looking for girls with wooden legs.[3]

Her work, for many, is hard to stomach; for others, it is a way to soar past the niceties of religiosity and soft-centered theology and hit pay dirt in what O'Connor calls the land of the "Christ-haunted." There is no room for whipped-cream clouds or pie-in-the-sky thinking within the hard clay ground of her stories. They resonate more with the philosophy that "the truth will set you free," though they're steeped in the reality of bright-eyed hypocrites and roadside sociopaths.

My own ears perked up when I heard my daughter Ginny, in conversation with her well-read, a-few-years-her-senior friend and mentor, refer to this author as "Saint Flannery." I wanted to know more. I had read some Flannery O'Connor in high school, including the story "Good Country People," but had fled rather quickly from that scene, haunted by visions of girls named "Hulga" with wooden legs and deviant Bible salesmen. My daughter, however, was so taken with O'Connor that she deemed her saint-worthy. This was worth checking out. And so I did. And, truth be told, reading this sharp-witted, no-holds-barred writer of the "Christ-haunted" South is not for the feint of heart or the weak of stomach. Dipping one's toe into a story like "A Good Man Is Hard to Find," thinking, "How can this be so bad with a title like that?" and then walking away terrified, muttering to oneself, "She went there … she really went there" doesn't seem like the beatific beginnings of a glorified soul. But there is a ruthlessness in her roads to redemption, an unending clamor for the glimmer of the eternal, barely lit and scantily visible though it be. And so I will never fold the pages closed of a Flannery O'Connor story deeply calmed and interminably relieved, but I will discover that there is a knot of challenge erupting in my soul, forever disrupting and interrupting my business as usual, her words of purpose echoing in my ears: "To the hard of hearing you shout, and for the almost-blind you draw large and startling figures."[4] And so she does.

Walking and Waking in the City of Olympia

"I can, with one eye squinted, take it all as a blessing."
—*The Habit of Being: Letters of Flannery O'Connor*

Downtown Olympia wouldn't normally be my choice for a meditative walk. Or really, any metro area. When I think of connecting with Spirit and my own mellow-yellowed or tangled-up insides, I usually crave an icing-smooth sandy beach, a cool quiet forest, or the predictability of a run-of-the-mill neighborhood with a few front yard maples rattling their lovely leafy confetti for good measure. These walks are melting moments for me. Connective moments. I want a place that will provide colorful decorations for my interior contemplative closet or at least soft ground to help cushion the fall.

I won't find that in Olympia today. Or at least I don't think I will. My brief history with this town includes a strange jumble of darkly roasted coffee, tumbling litter, and lobbyists proclaiming their beliefs on pin-back buttons. I've also encountered a swarm of tattooed and backpacked twenty-somethings chattering in groups of three or four in an abandoned city lot, colorful hairdos complementing rainbow-sprayed walls. Scenes like these arouse curiosity, even delight, but not contemplation.

I've read Flannery O'Connor's words—*I can, with one eye squinted, take it all as a blessing*—and am determined to squint. I want to find beauty here today, in this place, somewhere between the Capitol building and the Volcano Vapor Café. Somewhere in the midst of Buck's 5th Avenue Culinary Exotica shop and a place called Green Lady Marijuana.

To do this, I need to be open to side streets and nudges. I peel off State Street and move toward Percival

Landing, the waterfront area where the echoing voices of Salish Sea natives, cannery workers, and nineteenth-century ladies of the night may still be floating somewhere across the water. I look left and turn toward a potential eyesore. It is a half-paved alleyway with a lumpy seam of tar running down its middle, green tufts of weeds bulging from broken openings. Not my usual walking fare. But upon closer scrutiny, a sliver of a planter appears amid the cracked pavement. It holds the most golden marigold I've ever seen. Nestled nearby is some sweet-smelling rosemary. I enjoy the fragrance left on the whorls of my fingertips. *What a treat!* I think. *I would not have found this if I had been left to my usual devices.* Someone plotted out the plants and the colorful blooms in this box, probably hoping that a passerby like me would discover them. And I did! I suddenly feel lucky.

Turning toward Fourth Street, I am startled by loud music pulsating from windows in a passing car. *Wait!* I say to myself. *Listen this time.* A different rhythm, a different style, a different beat. I kind of like it, actually. I could get into this. I have on a different set of ears today, a new set of eyes; squinting or not, I'm seeing as I haven't before.

There is a trio of sidewalk sandwich boards at my right as I continue to wander. A person can tell, store by store, row by row, that these have been created with care and hopefulness: a stylized cup etched out in Chinese good-luck red, stenciled teddy bears and tin soldiers lined up within a matrix of pictures and words—someone thinking, someone crafting, to try to catch my eye. I can sense that there is a story behind each endeavor.

Up ahead, someone has dressed up a shop window. It's advertising a play production. The costumes shown are color-coordinated, era matching, and set up in height like a family of origin photograph, clothing the headless mannequins in some form of magic stagecraft. Someone else, across the street, in front of the bank, planted bright button clusters of mums, organized in clumps of purple, white, yellow, and orange. There's a little girl in a diaphanous blue dress, skin like black sand, sparkling in the sunlight as she crosses the street holding her father's hand. *I can . . . take it all as a blessing.*

I am noticing things more closely with *one eye squinted.* There are marks of care everywhere—those little things we humans tend to do to make a difference either for ourselves or for the soulful passerby.

More visions strike me: a double set of wooden doors, carved with hundreds of whimsical key shapes, crystal beveled glass adorning the top of a relic of a last-century building, the mint-green paint—a pretty choice—that outlines an unmarked storefront, its windows blinking brightly in front of tired white blinds.

A twenty-something girl approaches me and asks for change. Her fading acne and jack-o'-lantern eyes still hold a touch of innocence. I hand her a couple of quarters and am grateful to have felt a small taste of her being.

I see a large sign tucked into a corner of the city: Maddox and Laffoon, Attorneys at Law. I laugh to myself, *great names!*

Rhythm and Rye on a plastered poster—someone will be drumming tonight, making music. I can almost hear it in anticipation, pulsing from somewhere inside.

I hear myself saying, *One eye squinting, the other wide open.* Hmm … maybe that's how it's done. Or maybe that's how it happens. One eye slivered and focused, the other rapt with wonder.

A knickknack polar bear—the cute round snowballs of its backside face me from a second-story office window, and the silliness and curiosity of the possible story behind it give me a thrill. A woman up ahead of me sports a blouse and hair that blend in so beautifully with the fall; her golden waves and soft patterns of orange, brown, and yellow are hardly distinguishable from the turning maples surrounding us. An aged woman is writing in curves at her desk, carefully scribing each word with a slow movement of wrist and fingers. The fingerprints are everywhere. Interesting. Intentional. Inventive.

In the midst of a hard city, with one eye squinting, there is a soft center. *I can … take it all as a blessing.*

Likely or Unlikely Saint?
A Sitting Meditation

"The truth does not change according
to our ability to stomach it."

—*The Habit of Being: Letters of Flannery O'Connor*

There have been some truly heart-rending, soul-piercing, body-surrendering, harrowing moments in my life that, frankly, I wouldn't step back in line for and ask for second or third helpings. Yes, moments of enlightenment on our timeless time lines do appear, all glorious, symmetrical, and synchronistic in magnificent color schemes, but not usually during the bloodbath. During those moments, a good friend of mine says, "We hold a newly found wrench up to the sky and beg for mercy, while we fish around for another lost tool in the pool of our own despair." I know, that sounds dramatic, but oh, so truthful, doesn't it? Over time, I've learned that a fully loaded toolbox, though it does not guarantee success, can certainly quell the panic by good measure when needed.

The outright shocking images that gestate in the writing of Flannery O'Connor, messy wet afterbirth and all, are reminders of the dangerously beautiful world we all live in. We all float on the dreams of our ancestors, but enter through the birth canals of labor pangs, physical travail, and screams for oxygen. But once "out there" in the sea of our own humanity, we experience times of such pure goodness and incandescent beauty that we wouldn't have unless we lived out the risk of being human. The best of us, the worst of us, have that something—even for the tiniest fleck or speck of time—that we exhibit as signs of divinity. It may be found in a twinge of recognition that something *is* beautiful, something *is* precious. Or in the tiniest act of dignity or kindness shown to anything flickering with life. And *that* is where Flannery O'Connor shines amid the grotesque unravelings of characters that make her readers want to look away. It can be hard to stomach the truth, but somewhere deep within it, packed mud and rocks scratched diligently away, a tiny gem just might appear.

And it takes deep diligence, faith, and resilience to work your way through Flannery O'Connor's stories. You swallow many stones to get down to the rich, loamy earth. And then the bedrock.

When I picture this likely or unlikely saint, this Lady of the Christ-Haunted, I see a woman whose feet are planted several layers beneath the surface of topsoil. Her ankles are caked in the mud of reality, but her soles have made contact with substratum. In her hand is a tiny glimmer, a mere wink of light, but within it is the weight of the eternal. It shines like the north star at times, yet barely blinks out a pale glow in the inkiness of night at others.

I want this, and so I say, and so I pray: May my feet stand stalwart in the deep clay of the real, while holding on, with all my tenacity, all my ability, to the shining glimmer of all that is good, all that is beautiful, all that is eternal.

Amen.

Camino Divina Adventure: Into the Surprising

Where are the places in your surroundings that feel caked in mud or weighed down by the rocks and debris of hard or intense living? I'll bet they don't appear to be contemplative spaces to navigate, but they may surprise you. It might be the rock-hard and cemented place where the most tenacious sprig of grass or tangle of wildflowers somehow pokes through.

Speed-walking through a train station at rush hour, or meandering along the streets of an urban center's downtown, moving amid the distracted, stressed, and animated students at a university, standing inside the frenetic ruckus of a community event, such as a parade or a protest: Do you think it is possible *with one eye squinted* to find bits and pieces of beauty in any or all of these places? The challenge in today's *camino divina* adventure is to do just that—to find the lovely and surprising amid the "noise" of frenetic energy, quiet neglect, ugly indifference, and even pain.

Where will you go? If you live in or near a city, that's a natural. If you don't, where can you place yourself to be close to the potential of eclipsed surprise? Where can you safely wander, staying very aware of your surroundings but taking notice of hidden grace and elegance?

Make a list of those possible places, if you'd like, and then choose one.

Keeping Flannery O'Connor's statement in mind—"I can, with one eye squinted, take it all as a blessing"—begin your adventure. As you walk along, intentionally choose to turn a different direction in the road or take a side trip you normally wouldn't. Please be safe. Picking places in broad daylight or where there are lots of people is usually smart. What do you see? Does anything surprise you? Look closely. Does something draw you in with delight? I once heard a great spiritual teacher say to "follow the shimmer." Is something catching your eye with a glint of hope or possibility?

Continue your walk. Take another turn, whether down another side street or back onto the main drag. Within your current surroundings, is there something or someplace that appears particularly downtrodden or neglected? As you look very closely for a moment, can you see any signs of life or beauty that can be found there? An old layer of paint from days of glory, a small plant pushing through a dark corner, a glimmer of light in a place of darkness …

And notice people as well. As you see them pass by, what glimpses of beauty can you appreciate about each one of them? The details of facial expressions, textures of clothing, color of skin or hair? It may be physical or just their ways of being in the world. Children can be particularly delightful to notice. I remember hearing somewhere that to know something, you must first choose to love it. What will you choose to love today?

THE LONGER WALK

Deeper Dive

Flannery O'Connor is reported to have said, "You will know the truth and the truth will make you odd." That statement echoes my firm belief that whatever doesn't kill you makes you stranger (in the best sense of the word). And yet, sometimes the odd, the strange, or the unfamiliar creates twists and turns in our internal compass that can shake us and move us forward in ways that wouldn't have in the paths of the usual. Here are a few of Flannery O'Connor's words to get you started or keep you going:

> In yourself right now is all the place you've got.

> The way to despair is to refuse to have any kind of experience.

> It is better to be young in your failures than old in your successes.

> Grace changes us and change is painful.

> The life you save may very well be your own.

> Only if we are secure in our beliefs can we see the comical side of the universe.

> Faith is what someone knows to be true whether they believe it or not.

"What Is Found": Into the Surprising

My own
tangled-up insides crave
icing-smooth
melting moments,
connective moments,
colorful decorations for my
interior contemplative closet,
soft visual ground to help cushion the fall.

"I can, with one eye squinted,
take it all as a blessing"
somewhere between the Capitol building
and the Volcano Vapor Café.
Somewhere in the midst of
Buck's 5th Avenue Culinary Exotica shop
and a place called Green Lady Marijuana.

I am open to side streets and nudges—
a half-paved alleyway, a lumpy seam of tar,
green tufts of weeds, bulging broken openings.
I suddenly feel lucky—
the most golden marigold I've ever seen,
a stylized cup etched out in Chinese good-luck red,
a little girl in a diaphanous blue dress, skin like black
sand,
a double set of wooden doors, carved with hundreds
of whimsical keys.

I hear myself saying,
"One eye squinting, the other wide open."

The fingerprints are everywhere.
Interesting. Intentional. Inventive.

In the midst of a hard city, there is a soft center.

"I can ... take it all as a blessing."

The Scalloped Path

Whether unpeeling the layers of the city or the deep strata of Flannery O'Connor's writing, it feels important to carefully display the newly uncovered and sometimes difficult discoveries with rich conversation and an ear to the subtle. As you gather together your encounters and revelations of the day, allow the prize of surprise and new appreciation to be unveiled.

1. Tell the story, step-by-step, that led you to a surprising discovery on your *camino divina* adventure. How did it surprise you? Did you discover any layers to what you found that were invisible at first glance?

2. What were a few of the other unforeseen or eye-opening treats you came across? What characteristic(s) drew you into the "shimmer"?

3. Did you have an especially difficult encounter that made it particularly challenging to find beauty or delight? If so, describe it. Were you able to eventually find either of the two—beauty or delight? Or something else? What did you find?

4. What new places, nooks, or corners did you discover on your somewhat serendipitous saunter? Will you go back to any of your newly found haunts?

5. What did you learn—ugly or beautiful, dark or luminous—about yourself today? Did it surprise you?

Suggested Readings

Gooch, Brad. *Flannery: A Life of Flannery O'Connor*. New York: Back Bay Books, 2010.

A biography illuminated by interviews and a recent cache of unsealed letters.

O'Connor, Flannery. *The Complete Stories*. New York: Farrar, Straus and Giroux, 1971.

Winner of the National Book Award and guaranteed to make your skin and your soul crawl.

O'Connor, Flannery. *Mystery and Manners: Occasional Prose*. New York: Farrar, Straus and Giroux, 1969.

A collection of her essays, articles, and lectures resurrected after her death.

O'Connor, Flannery. *A Prayer Journal by Flannery O'Connor*. Edited by W. A. Sessions. New York: Farrar, Straus and Giroux, 2013.

Early and intimate encounters with O'Connor's spiritual dialogue.

Wood, Ralph C. *Flannery O'Connor and the Christ-Haunted South*. Grand Rapids, MI: Wm. B. Eerdmans Publishing Co., 2005.

A chance to explore the culture of the "Christ-haunted" South through her theological lens.

Chapter 11

An Adventure into Connectivity

Chief Seattle—Brother of Webbed Theology

He was born at the Old-Man-House Village on the Black River to the "people of the clear salt water" as well as "the people of the inside" and "the people of the big lake," known collectively as the Suquamish and the Duwamish tribes. He was called Si'ahl or Sealth or Seattle by his own people. He was known as "Le Gros" or "The Big One" by Hudson Bay Company traders. And he was baptized "Noah" by a priest in the Roman Catholic Church. As you can probably guess, the naming of things wove some complex strands into the web of life of this Northwest *tyee*, or chief.

The naming of a great city by the Salish Sea, also called the Puget Sound, is attributed to Dr. David Maynard. Reportedly a good friend of Chief Seattle and owner of a trading post along the shores of the Duwamish River, "Doc" decided to name the newly emerging city after his Suquamish/Duwamish friend. According to writer Peter Stekel, "The Tyee was less than pleased with the distinction, convinced as he was that, after dying, every time Seattle was spoken he would turn in his grave."[1]

As the scrambling for lands and the scrabbling for territories out West occurred more and more in the mid-nineteenth century, the nomenclature of native place and the translation of tribal word were often scratched out recklessly in flourishes not necessarily true to their original forms. Hence, there is much controversy about the accuracy of Chief Seattle's famous and generously quoted speech that begins with the words: "Yonder sky that has wept tears of compassion on our fathers for centuries untold, and which, to us, appears changeless and eternal, may change." Surgeon Dr. Henry J. Smith was there to document a "fragment of his speech" and published it in an article written for *The Seattle Sunday Star* on October 29, 1887, over thirty years after the event. It was probably translated from Seattle's Lush-ootseed tongue into what was called Chinook Jargon, or *chinuk wawa*, a pidgin trade language, and then finally into English. Regardless of translation precision or lack thereof, Smith states regarding the chief that "neither his eloquence, his dignity or his grace were acquired. They were as native to his manhood as leaves and blossoms are to a flowering almond." In other words, he had presence beyond words.

My own moment gracefully caught in the web of Chief Seattle's elegance was when I first read this statement:

> Humankind has not woven the web of life. We are but one thread within it. Whatever we do to the web, we do to ourselves. All things are bound together. All things connect.[2]

The idea of human community was grandly stepping forth into my consciousness at that time, and Chief Seattle provided the great hoop that held me there. I hadn't before found a weaving of words catch me so netlike in the eloquence of their meaning, yet so practically, silkily, luxuriously in the fibers of their form. I guess you could say, in a world of sometimes reckless thoughts and titles, he provided a naming ceremony.

Weaving and Unwinding along Deception Pass

"Man did not weave the web of life,
he is merely a strand in it."
—From a speech in 1854

From my small Euclidean matrix of neighborhood, I ride along the spine of my island, Route 525, to the crookneck turn that takes me to Highway 20 across the Deception Pass bridge and on to Rosario Beach State Park. Whether I've been thinking about it or not, I've been floating along on an invisible map, noticed mainly by blinking satellites and soaring birds of prey. I get my own view of this every now and then when I'm on an airplane, glimpsing green squares and golden circles of farmland connected by blue veins of aqueducts as well as the dazzling circuitry of computer chip cities below, flashing red and white with the ever-flow of moving head- and taillights.

I tiptoe down from the heights of my friend's truck and enter another map, another web. Like all topography, there are bumps and ridges. As I begin to walk along the main trail, trees appear as straight lines—a vertical matrix reminding me that the planes of existence aren't just below my feet but also lie in lofty layers all around me. At this moment, I even recall the concept of ley lines—that there may be rivers of energy that flow beneath us noticed by the likes of migrating birds and highly intuitive humans.

I hold these words in my mental pocket: *Man did not weave the web of life* ... By carrying them along with me, I am more deeply aware of the webbings and patterns within my visual sphere: tangles of curling branches mixed with dangling strands of newborn leaves, more weave than confusion, webbings of light below in the water creating soft pentagons and hexagons reverberating on rocks and sand, the lace of froth and foam tatting an edge on the shoreline; millions of spindles of dry pine, softening the understory of time and forest under its rusty blanket.

The map of existence. The topography of our days. *The web of life*.

Along this micro-atlas of western Washington, I scan the trail's surface and its environs, finding that root meets root in a gentle grid of fibrous elegance. I imagine that the moss dripping in lush cascades from a nearby tree may be someone's airy green loft. A dandelion appears; it could be an umbrella of shade for a passing ant or a wandering beetle. Even the open bursts of burls and scars on a tree branch will inevitably create a hosting site for many sets of wandering legs and wings. Though I trample on the remnants of broken branches and the tiny carcasses of life itself too small to notice, I can feel this is a benevolent web. A beneficent world. A big-hearted map.

When I stop moving, I sense a web of sound, too. Lap and splash beneath the crest of the cliff create a smooth bass line upon which a threshing bird plays its own counter-rhythm. Sound strands pearl along the strand, the margin between beach and bay, humming from somewhere amid the gush of waves in an asymmetrical rhythm. What gentle sonic breath can I add to the song? What pulse can I beat alongside this ever-weaving sonata of living? And, I realize, I am doing these things just by being alive, just by being here. I am a part of the unfolding composition of sound and life-scape.

A small bird's twitter from the great "out there" adds undulating piccolo. Beyond the resounding honk of a lone goose is the slow simmer of life, punctuated suddenly by a child's jubilant scream. I trace the underlying tempo of it all with this motion: 11111111—and another aviary musician shows up to add a delicate *djembe* beat as well.

When I stop to think about it, webs are all around me. Bloodlines that pump from one generation into the next, scattering histories and gene pools across the surface of humankind. Scallops of pinecone scales harbor seeds that will bloom into hearty woodland flowers where birds, water, and wind will take them to places only the soil will know. Webs of shadow entwine my existence with every other shape that inhabits these unfolding rays of sun—my body blending with rock. My head, now a part of a mountain. My torso and limbs, the twins of trees.

This invigorates me.

He is merely a strand, Chief Seattle's words continue.

Being out here, it is easy to be a strand. I see no reason to stand out, stomp around, or lord over other creatures. Being a glistening fiber in the delicate web is a lovely enough thing. A community thing. A together thing.

We are all silver sometimes when the sun hits us right. We are all shadow when it does not.

Nearby, long strands of thick sap make a tree's own interior honey drip slowly into an amber crust, a petrified jewel. Lengthy peels of madrona, red on green, dry on raw, make me think of summer days when I dropped my own layers of skin, exfoliating the old, making ready for the new. These are all strands as well. Strands of beauty. Strands of memory. They take me down my own trail of personal maps and webs. I think about the bones of others that weave the pasts that create the nests we currently live in, the nets of hope we float upon.

This preserve feels like a floating place. The inlets are a confection of blue, weaving an aerial pattern of tributaries and connections; the large web of walkways buoyant above the glowing coastline. Deep down I know I want all things to work together. Like honeycombs and nursing logs. Symbiotically. Weblike. Complementing each other in this womb of sunlight. *Man did not weave the web of life, he is merely a strand in it.*

In a final eye-pan of forested beauty, I take in green nourishment from eyes to soul. The tapestry, the matrix, the web weaves itself before me. I am both warp and weft within it.

Likely or Unlikely Saint?
A Sitting Meditation

"If we do not own the freshness of the air and the sparkle of the water, how can you buy them?"

—From a letter to President
Franklin Pierce in 1855

I recall reading somewhere a fragrant sage-y thought: not only do you remember a place, but a place also remembers you. Your presence somewhere in a state of just *being* over and over again makes subtle and deep impressions on the landscape. You eventually become a familiar entity, a part of the spatial community, beloved even. Perhaps not surprisingly, the place becomes a part of you, too, sinking into your own personal place-ness as well.

I used to contemplate this idea when I visited a local wilderness park almost weekly. *How am I becoming a*

*friend and familiar to this place of peeling eucalyptus, this
pooling flow of oak leaves, this skyline edged with hawk's
cry? Will they remember me? Will it remember me? Miss me?*
Whenever I go back to Bell's Canyon and its environs,
I still can somehow feel myself there, as if I never left,
now incredibly and indelibly a part of that landscape.

I think a gift Chief Seattle gives to me, and maybe
to you as well, is a sense of community. Each and
every one part and parcel of everything. True community. And in the spirit of that community comes a
chance to give from what we have and who we are;
to bestow our gifts on the great intertribal potlatch
of a place. The bounty is simple: a playfully dropped
cone from the nearby Jeffrey pine, a distant but luscious melt of pink sunset along the western horizon,
a gentle song sung in a spirit of gratitude, a loving and
peaceful presence.

When I imagine Chief Seattle as Brother of Webbed
Theology, likely or unlikely saint, I can see him in his
beloved place near forest and river on Suquamish land.
His hands are filled with familiar gifts: thimbleber-
ries, salmonberries, basket-making coiled cedar roots,
the rough shells of tender clams—gifts of place, gifts
of community. He wears a robe of lacy spiderweb, the
filaments and fibers intricate and decorated with dew
and sun. As he stretches out his arms, which culminate
in open palms, the gifts drop out, and the web of life
expands. In it there is a multiplicity of living things
spreading out for all to see, crawling, weaving, bursting

forth within a web of gathering—a community of inter-connection in well-woven splendor.

I want this, too, and so I pray, and so I say: May I hold the gifts of my own unique life in the palms of my hands, spreading them onto the places and spaces that call me home, while wearing the mantle of our beloved shared existence.

Amen.

Camino Divina Adventure: Into Connectivity

There are rivers, roads, and tributaries of connection all around us. Webs and spirals and echoes everywhere. And we are a part of this swirling motion, this sea of connectivity. As you begin your *camino divina* adventure today, start by taking a closer look at the circuitry that shapes your world the moment you step out of bed. Try to create a mental picture of the physicality of your paths from place to place—bedroom to kitchen, kitchen to living room, living room to car or bike, road or path to destination, filled with right turns, left turns, roundabouts. Do it in dot-to-dot fashion, or with a big, fat mental permanent marker outlining your steps from place to place. What does the pattern look like? A labyrinth, a pencil maze, an M. C. Escher drawing? Something else? What is the shape of your movement connections? Draw it, if you'd like. You might be struck dumb in an admiring stupor of the connections you create with feet and tire all the time.

Now imagine the circles of connection you are a part of. Think of them in your mind's eye like echo patterns after a stone has been dropped in a pool of water. What people connections begin with you, then ripple out to other layers of the circle, other rings of the tree of life, further and further expanding, and then creating tangential circles that may overlap like a mandorla or a Venn diagram? Write them down if you'd like. Create a connectivity map. It's fun to watch it all unfold. Are there other kinds of connections in your life that do the same thing, rippling out in echo form? Those of place? Or idea?

Now that you've connected through the skeins of your imagination into your personal web of life, step out there and find the strands that weave the broad and beyond parts together as well. Wherever you choose to go, in the circumference of your neighborhood or city, or within the perimeters of a state or county park, look for the details of connection—in the symbiotic relationships of things as well as in the chain reactions of their activities. Where does the white-crowned sparrow land? What does she do once she does? How has her inhabitance there affected the tree, beneficially and detrimentally? What does the tree look like? Where are its grooves and notches? Who is living there now? What circumstances may its scars and hollows connect to? How do tree and creature inhabiting it connect to the sky? To the earth? To you? How does viewing all of this benefit you? What interior trails does this viewing take you on? What metaphors or images come up for you? What spirals, echoes, and webs do you see right now?

Or as you enter a complex cityscape, how does a skyscraper connect to a matrix of buildings, connect to the greater metropolitan area, connect to "on the outskirts"? How do you walk them together with your being, your own life-scape? How are you a connector in your daily living in the realms of work, relationships, volunteerism, play, or exploration? How are you part of the web of life? How are you a weaver and connecting point in the web of your own life as well as the lives of others? Sit with these questions for a while. Try to answer them, and journal about them, too, if you'd like.

How are you *merely a strand in it*?

THE LONGER WALK

Deeper Dive

The circles spiraling within the web of life line up much like the layers of ancient tree rings—both are tangible testaments to the expanding universe of depth and diligence. Connecting closer to the world around you and the worlds within you is often a matter of time. Time invested in a relationship with either creates all the more growth rings, producing a stronger, heavier body of living. Spending a few more moments with the words of Chief Seattle can help to do just that.

> Take only memories; leave nothing but footprints.

> All things share the same breath—the beast, the tree, the man.

There is no death, only a change of worlds.

Earth does not belong to us; we belong to earth.

Day and night cannot dwell together.

The soil is rich with the life of our kindred.

"What Is Found": Into Connectivity

Euclidean matrix, spine of island,
crookneck turn—
I'm floating on an invisible map,
noticed by blinking satellites,
birds of prey.

Planes of existence lie in lofty layers,
a vertical matrix, ley lines.

"Man did not weave the web of life …"
is the understory of time,
the topography of our days.

In a gentle grid of fibrous elegance,
in the lush cascades of airy green lofts of moss,
in the open bursts of burls and scars,
I feel a benevolent web,
a beneficent world,
a big-hearted map.

Sound strands pearl along the strand—
what can I add to the song?
the unfolding composition of sound
and life-scape?

We are all silver sometimes.
We are all shadow.
Strands of beauty.
Strands of memory.

The bones of others
weave the pasts, the nets
we float upon.

In a final eye-pan of beauty,
I take it in, eyes to soul:
the web weaves before me.

I am both warp and weft
within it.

The Scalloped Path

A potlatch or "giveaway" is a gathering ceremony where West Coast tribes come together to redistribute the wealth garnered throughout the prosperous seasons. Drawing close as a talking community to redistribute the wealth of experience and story is also a form of sharing treasured and valuable gifts. Here are some questions to help ignite the fire, gather in a circle, and lay out your banquet of words.

1. Describe some of the webs of life or circles of connection you may have discovered on your *camino divina* journey. Did any of them strike a particular note of poignancy or resonance for you? How?
2. What strands of beauty did you find? Were any of them surprising? Or not what you expected at first glance?
3. Share some of the circles of living of which you are a part. Do any of them connect to or reverberate with other circles?
4. What are some of the ripples you are experiencing from the interconnections you are currently a part of? If they are joyful, what makes them so? If they are challenging,

how do you see them incorporated possibly and eventually into a sea of good outcomes?

5. In your current state, as a strand in the web of life, if you were to take your thread and spin it outward, where do you see it taking you? Where would you like it to take you?

Suggested Readings

Ankele, Daniel, Denise Ankele, and Edward Curtis, photographers. *Edward Curtis: Pacific Northwest Tribes—285+ Native American Indian Photographs* (only available on Kindle). Grover Beach, CA: Ankele Publishing, 2014.

A beautiful photographic look at Northwest tribes through the eyes of portraitist Edward Curtis.

Jefferson, Warren. *The World of Chief Seattle: How Can One Sell the Air?* Summertown, TN: Native Voices Books, 2001.

Written in cooperation with the Suquamish tribe, this book provides some context to Chief Seattle's place within the web of life.

Nerburn, Kent. *The Wisdom of the Native Americans*. Novato, CA: New World Library, 1999.

A collection of quotations, speeches, and sage words from America's first nations.

Chapter 12

An Adventure into the Liminal

Annie Dillard—Anchorite of Bells and Wings

Meta Ann Doak, known to most of the rest of the world as Annie Dillard, was the "spiritually promiscuous" firstborn daughter of Frank and Pamela Doak—he, a passionate joke-teller and she, a practical joke dealer (among other things). They made way for a daughter who was an early-on immersive risk-taker, both in her inner and outer worlds. In her memoir *An American Childhood*, she states, "You can't test courage cautiously, so I ran hard and waved my arms hard, happy."

Brought up in the Point Breeze neighborhood of Pittsburgh, Pennsylvania, she spent her time reading books like Ann Haven Morgan's *A Field Guide to Ponds and Streams*, S. I. Hayakawa's *The Story of Language*, and Ralph Waldo Emerson's *Essays*, and listening to C. S. Lewis's broadcasts on theology. She tried drag racing, smoking cigarettes (which got her suspended from school), and hanging with the Beat poets, bongos in hand. When her parents and headmistress wanted to send her off to college in the South to smooth out her rough edges, she writes in her memoir, "I had hopes for my rough edges. I wanted to use them as a can opener, to cut myself a hole in the world's surface and exit through it."[1]

She wrote the collection of poems *Tickets for a Prayer Wheel* in 1974, but the literary world really seemed to wake up to her genius and insight when *Pilgrim at Tinker Creek* was published that same year and ended up winning the Pulitzer Prize. It was also considered one of the *New York Times*'s "Best 100 Nonfiction Books of the Twentieth Century."

Her subsequent works, such as *Holy the Firm*, *Teaching a Stone to Talk*, *An American Childhood*, and *The Writing Life* are well loved and acclaimed, but I always go back to walking those richly soiled paths of Virginia's Roanoke Valley along with her in *Pilgrim at Tinker Creek*. This book was my first encounter with Annie Dillard, and my eyes were flung wide open, lids slightly flapping in prose astonishment. "*What*?! How can she talk about such beauty, ugliness, and pain interwoven into such a delicacy of sentence structure so that I'm smitten and terrified at the same time?!" Perhaps a bit of an overstatement. But her work was my first encounter with nature as "beauty tangled in a rapture with violence," no longer *Mutual of Omaha's Wild Kingdom* dressed up in its Sunday best (or was it?). It did take me down the road of the *real* as I had never traversed it before. And that's what *real* is, right? A layer of excruciating pain that brings you down into a layer of exhilarating beauty that drops you further into an appreciation of excruciating depth, which again leads you somehow to inexplicable joy.

I had never seen this splayed out on the page before. The specimens of life pinned onto corkboard, displayed in all their gorgeousness and exasperation: luminosity, fluorescence, raggedness, fragility, and ephemeralness. Yet I know that in many ways, this is also the experience of my own life, in all its tattered, rugged, and radiant glory.

Edging the Gaps at Ebey's Bluff

> "The gaps are the thing. The gaps are
> the spirit's one home …"
>
> *—Pilgrim at Tinker Creek*

Funny how the Ebey's Bluff trail starts at a cemetery, its headstones bellowing out lost names in cement brocade. It feels like beginning at the end. But somehow that seems appropriate for Annie Dillard's words scribbled in my hand—*The gaps are the thing. The gaps are the spirit's one home …*—because I find so many gaps here: the moment between life and death, the passage between life and afterlife, the twinkling of an eye between here and there. To those of us who wrestle, or toy with, or wholeheartedly embrace thoughts of heaven or the next life, the space-gaps in the graveyard almost seem like hiccups in time, holes dug out where the seed was placed, the hull that once surrounded personal essence, now coddled with dirt and sod, hoping the invisible sprout will journey on. *The gaps are the thing.* Gaps temporarily filled. Gaps gaping with open mouths, open jaws, open arms. Gaps anticipating the next human seed.

It seems like a sobering place to start a journey, and it is, but not completely. Walking in a landscape of my own intentional silence, the interiors are bubbling and in constant motion. The valley below the bluff is checkered with farm fields in colors of amber and emerald. There is a joy to all of this, both the bubbling thoughts and the silence of the serene scene. And there is a gap even here, between this "time out of time" opportunity on a small trail near Route 525 and the town of Coupeville, which leads me back to everyday life; that philosophical gap between hiking trails and highways.

Moving along the edges of this bluff, I continue to notice gaps everywhere: in the space between the rustic logs of a historic blockhouse, in the charred fireplace flue of an old cabin, and in the underhousing crawl space there that's teeming with mystery, filled with invisible stories. Spaces, spaces everywhere, and more than a drop to think. Gaps aplenty. Gaps in the human-built world. Gaps in the natural world.

I ask myself, how are they a home? How are the gaps home?

I look up. The sky above me, with all of its cloudy etheric shapes, is a gap between earth and outer galaxy.

Between myself and the water's edge, bleeding with eye-blinding light up ahead of me, lies a gap between here and there. And I find that as I breathe——*in-breath, out-breath*——there is a gap poised between the drafts of air coming in and the carbon dioxide going out. At the very top of the breath, a stopping point, neither inhale nor release. Is that the spirit's home? And why does Spirit want to live there?

A white butterfly looks like a folded napkin flapping against the blue tablecloth of sky. A large chunk of granite boasts cracks up and down its ancient spine. Wildflowers pop up where other plants choose not to. Pockets of warm air emerge between the quiet spaces, potent on a chilly day.

"Where are you?" I ask. I am walking the gaps today. I want to know *the spirit's one home.* I can almost hear an answer. "Filling in. Being the 'everywhere.' Holding up the kestrel in her flight; staying between the known and the unknown; aren't you glad Somebody's there?"

Whose spirit is speaking? My spirit? The Spirit? Is there much of a difference?

I look down again. A dandelion releases its stars, leaving its stalk of green body behind, the last bits of constellation clinging to its old life. Both circumstances are beautiful, the leaving and the staying, the floating and the lingering, for comfort, for life quest. The trees above me look like lightning bolts, bared branches naked and jagged, striking the air, yet frozen and inverted on the earth. Or are they totem poles, uncarved, commemorating this place, this space on our natural history time line? Either way, they bridge the gap between soil and sky. They are mythical ladders between here and there. My eyes follow a troupe of tiny birds swooping in a mass twitter of sound from bush to bush. They are safely navigating the gaps between start point and end point, the naked space between landing and landing. Watching them transverse these small expanses together brings me joy.

A bald eagle appears above, soaring through the great "Gap of Sky" with confidence, giving it the feeling of opportunity rather than unfilled space.

Within this interlude of silence, I now remember the idea of "negative space." An artist friend of mine back in California would often tell me that the quiet shapes formed by the space surrounding an object are just as important as the object itself. It is the ability to have a concurrent awareness of both form and nonform that makes this idea work—what's there and what supports what's there. The substance of gaps. I suppose she might agree: *The gaps are the thing.*

I finish my walk on Ebey's Bluff trail at the same place where I began. The stones of memory are still erected there but the form of the unseen creates the shapes that hold them in place. And I, too, am somehow held.

Likely or Unlikely Saint?
A Sitting Meditation

"What is important is the moment of opening a life
and feeling it touch—with an electric hiss and cry—
this speckled mineral sphere, our present world."

—*An American Childhood*

The term "anchorite," used primarily back in the Middle Ages, referred to a sacred soul whose chosen withdrawal from the tasks, rigors, and rhythms of daily life formed him or her into a hallowed hermit of sorts, *anchored* to the parish church via a miniature dwelling place, a pocket-sized connecting domicile. Often literally sealed in by a bishop who performed funereal rites for its inhabitant, the cell held a tiny viewing window opening up to the church's altar. This opening was also used as an aperture for the giving of wisdom and insight to those who visited the "living saint." There was another place within the dwelling, to slide simple meals in and bodily refuse out, and one last small opening that faced the broader world, exposing its inhabitant to a slight light entering the room through an opaque cloth, making the outside world seem that much more distant. The little cell or "anchorhold" became a symbolic womb for the spiritual community, holding within its walls the collected ideals of church and individual, the potentiality of rebirth in metaphor through the committed work of the pious one living within.

When I think of Annie Dillard as the "anchorite of bells and wings," I don't see her wearing a nun's habit, bearing a cowl or a scapular, but a woman consecrated in all-weather apparel and hiking boots. I see a person, a poet of ordinary and extraordinary time, committed to indwelling *this* world. I see her setting up shop in forest and ridge, holed up in a cabin on a weathered night, or tented near a vibrant world of wildlife and water; outside, yet alongside the rest of us, mining the depths of the underspoken—those things that cry out for the dressing and holy garb of words. In doing this, she notices the scant, the slight, the nearly invisible, and takes notes for us, getting her fingers dirty in the wonder, the "electric hiss and cry" of this "speckled mineral sphere," fondling the mystery and sharing the archaeology of its contours.

When I imagine the anchorite of bells and wings, this one who sees in "enormous wings ... bands of blue and pink delicate as a watercolour wash ... a fragility unfurled to strength,"[2] this resonant bell who didn't know it until she was "lifted and struck," I see a saint who has built with her own hands a domicile of clay, an earthenware home, a dome fired in the kiln of this sun-baked sphere, living alongside the walk of our daily lives. She is committed to communing with and contemplating the substance of soil and spirit. She holds in one hand the bell that wakes us up to the sonorous toll of our own layered and luscious reality. In the other, she holds the tools for fashioning a set of wings—not the frothy or frivolous, but the blueprinted kind engraved with flight patterns—of future, of present, in order to navigate the zephyrs and headwinds of this world.

And so I say, and so I pray: May I hold in my hands as well as in the depths of my own clay dwelling the clarion bell of who I am and who I am becoming with awake-ness and appreciation, while holding ever-ready the tools that teach me how to fly.

Amen.

Camino Divina Adventure: Into the Liminal

I have always been fascinated by liminal spaces, those places in the in-between, on the thresholds, or near the brink of entering unexplored territory; those hidden and nameless spheres that are neither here nor there but are on the way from there to the next here. These liminal times are often transitional and, at their best, transformational. They can be looked at as nowhere lands, but I've most often experienced them as every-where lands, as they can be places that teach us the wis-dom we need to take with us on the next part of our journeys.

A number of years ago, I wrote a poem marking this very doorstep into "time out of time" that began:

> Before you cross it today,
> pause.
> You are leaving the inside
> for the outside—

the safety of interiors
for the adventure
of exteriors,
the known, for the
unknown,

and ended:

Before you cross it today,
pause.

You are leaving the outside
for the inside.
The safety of the exteriors
for the adventure of the
interiors;
the known,
for the unknown.

As you make your way over your own threshold today and out into your personal beyond, know that you are not only tapping the riches available in the outside world, but you are tapping the riches of your inside world as well.

Today's adventure is all about discovering the gaps, the liminal spaces, the thresholds. The tools you will need for this journey are a pair of open eyes and the ability to press PAUSE. As you wander within your place of choice, which could be anywhere, look for the possible gaps and then be sure to pause; in doing this, you're taking the time to probe how spirit may dwell there.

Also, let this walk be in "slow time," a term John O'Donohue uses that connotes a more gradual, under-paced, self-tending period of time. Remember that walking *camino divina* isn't about doing an exercise, it's about mining the depths of time, space, and place, including what's inside yourself and beyond the borders of your own skin.

When you think about gaps, consider that they may be seemingly empty spaces in the physical world: the spaces between tree branches, the pockets of landscape where there is less fecundity or growth, or a hole or burrow in the ground. Once you've taken an initial look at these empty pockets, take a second look at them. This time, consider them as "negative spaces," the spaces that support and hold the more obvious parts of the landscape. In this new context, is there a difference in how you would describe those spaces now? If so, try to verbalize or write these thoughts down to clarify them further.

Gaps can be metaphorical "empty" spaces in the spiritual world as well—spaces that hold potential, possible knowledge, wisdom, or the unknown. What do you envision in these gaps? What could be in these "empty" places? Why do you think these spaces exist? If Spirit lives there, why does it? And what does Spirit create or provide in these places? Use what is called your "sacred imagination"—that place inside you that forms ideas from the clay of your own insight, wisdom, and intuition—to sculpt what is possible.

Now think about the potential thresholds that you may come across on your walk. Perhaps a fork in the road or stepping out of shadow into sun, or sun into shadow. Or maybe stepping into a cool, watery place out of an arid place or vice versa. Like these examples, look for the thresholds that open up to you along the way, the visible or invisible doorways that take you from one experience into another, from one microcosm or even macrocosm into another. Take notice of them and mark their transitions. *Your* transitions. Where might Spirit dwell here? Where might *your* spirit dwell on each side of the threshold or on the threshold itself? What is your spirit feeling or intuiting in these places?

Realize on this *camino divina* that lingering on thresholds can often produce more questions than answers. And that's OK. More than OK, because that's mostly what the gaps are for. Consider taking an artifact with you from one or more of the thresholds you cross or consider today—an acorn, a stone, a scrap of paper, a marker of any sort—to remind you of a question or realization that showed up on the threshold for you.

May your time on the thresholds and in the gaps bring you more spaciousness and more clarity, and in that clarity an awareness of the potential that awaits you.

THE LONGER WALK

Deeper Dive

In her book *Pilgrim at Tinker Creek*, Annie Dillard said, "I had been my whole life a bell, and never knew it until at that moment I was lifted and struck." The clarity of living, of being, is often found in the resonance that comes from experiencing, feeling the clapper move inside the silver cloche of who you are. Here are a few more wise words from Annie Dillard to get your imagination ringing loudly and clearly into the realm of experience.

> The silence is not suppression; instead, it is all there is.

> The secret of seeing is to sail on solar wind.

> I am a fugitive and a vagabond, a sojourner seeking signs.

> We live in all we seek.

> How we spend our days is, of course, how we spend our lives.

"What Is Found": Into the Liminal

> Beginning at the end.
> Gaps between life and death,
> life and afterlife, here and there,
> gaps that seem like hiccups in time.
> Gaps temporarily filled.
> Gaps anticipating the next human seed.
>
> Gaps everywhere—
> the sky above with all of its etheric shapes—

a gap between earth and outer galaxy.
As I breathe, *in-breath, out-breath,*
a gap poised at the very top of breath.
Is that the spirit's home?

White butterfly is a folded napkin
flapping against the blue tablecloth of sky.
A large chunk of granite boasts cracks up and down its
ancient spine.

"Where are you?" I ask.
I can almost hear an answer.
"Filling in. Being the 'everywhere.'
Holding up the kestrel in her flight;
staying between the known and the unknown;
aren't you glad Somebody's there?"

I look down again.
A dandelion releases its stars,
the last bits of constellation clinging to its old life.
The trees above me look like lightning strikes,
frozen and inverted on the earth.
They bridge the gap between soil and sky,
mythical ladders between here and there.

"The gaps are the spirit's one home ..."

An interlude of silence,
negative space—
shapes formed by surrounding,
awareness of form and nonform,
what's there and what supports what's there.
The substance of gaps ...

"The gaps are the things."
I, too, am somehow held.

The Scalloped Path

In her book *The Writing Life*, Annie Dillard explains that "the impulse to keep to yourself what you have learned is not only shameful, it is destructive. Anything you do not give freely and abundantly becomes lost to you. You open your safe and find ashes."[3] While to some that might sound histrionic, I think in most circumstances it rings true. The very act of sharing our experiences spreads the wealth, but also deepens the treasure inside ourselves. When the words are formed, then encouraged to step over the threshold and out into the world, the shapes of our thoughts become refined, and then memorialized in a sweet, rich way. I encourage you to take the time to send your words out into the world. Here are a few questions to start.

1. Were there any gaps or thresholds on your *camino divina* that especially caught your attention? Why? Describe in details or word pictures the threshold you found and the discoveries you made there.

2. How did the thresholds you found on your *camino divina* connect to thresholds you are now crossing in your daily life? What do you hope to find on the other side of the doorway? What do you think you might be leaving behind? What does it feel like to stand right there, on the threshold itself? What support can you envision that might help you work through the "in-between."

3. When you think of gaps, either found in nature or opening up in your personal or work life, what might your sacred imagination see filling them? Spirit? Potential? Mystery? Take some time, and maybe a little space

to form your own thoughts and pictures on this, either individually or with a partner, then come back together to share your ideas as a group.

4. On the longer *camino divina* continuum of your life, recall a few of the gaps and thresholds you have experienced. Then review your feelings at the time, and the support you sought, either within yourself or outside yourself. Were there people or experiences that helped fill in the gaps or at least walk you through them? How did that transition time resolve? What enlivening outcomes, if any, happened once you crossed the threshold? Who did you become?

Suggested Readings

Dillard, Annie. *An American Childhood*. New York: Harper & Row Publishers, 2013.

Exquisite writing detailing the iconic growing-up years of this author from Pittsburgh.

Dillard, Annie. *Mornings Like This*. New York: Harper Perennial, 1996.

A foundry of found poems concocted from a collection of book snippets—sometimes old, sometimes odd.

Dillard, Annie. *Pilgrim at Tinker Creek*. New York: Harper Perennial Modern Classics, 2007.

Observations within the landscape that take the reader down trails of metaphysical thought and interior insight; a Pulitzer Prize winner.

Dillard, Annie. *Teaching a Stone to Talk: Expeditions and Encounters*. New York: Harper Perennial, 2013.

A trek into this profoundly beautiful wordsmith's encounters, discoveries, and questions into the deep.

Dillard, Annie. *The Writing Life.* New York: Harper Perennial, 2013.

A book that shares with the reader the difficult, sometimes torturous, yet at times transcendent work of a writer.

Acknowledgments

I would like to thank Tricia Elisara and Jan Gough for insight on my Spanish usage, as well as heaps and gobs of deeply appreciated enthusiasm in general. Linda and Judy Mammano for listening and giving great encouragement in the early stages. Julie Mammano for helpful publishing-world words of wisdom. Ravi Verma for having faith in the potential of my writing. Fred Krueger for opening my eyes to "Opening the Book of Nature" and seeing place as a spiritual practice. For Younger Leader's Network and Montage for cultivating a seeding ground for all things creative and all things green. My special cadre of spiritual directors, lovingly known as "Scary Precious" for being the primordial goo that helped incubate me into the spiritual companion that I am. For Hope Lyda's consistent cheerleading, tinged with helpful humor from the sidelines. For Emily Wichland and the folks at SkyLight Paths Publishing for saying "yes!" and giving me the opportunity to literally walk out this project. For Ginny and John, my smart, creative, grown-up children who continue to loop the labyrinth of life with me. For my husband, Rick Vander Kam, an ever-amazing support and the biggest Gina Marie Mammano enthusiast of them all! For the kind and open friends, colleagues, and fellow-journeyers on Whidbey Island. And for my tribe of California women who have been trusted friends, threshold keepers, and shining stars in my galaxy for many, many years.

Notes

Introduction

1. John Muir, *Our National Parks* (Boston: Houghton Mifflin, 1901), 56.
2. John Muir, *John Muir: His Life and Letters and Other Writings*, ed. Terry Gifford (Seattle: Mountaineers Books, 1996), 96.
3. Gervase Holdaway, ed., *The Oblate Life* (Collegeville, MN: Liturgical Press, 2008), 109.
4. Ken Ludden, *Mystic Apprentice: Meditative Skills with Symbols and Glyphs Supplemental,* vol. 3 (Lulu.com, 2011), 17.

Chapter 1 An Adventure into the Familiar—Wendell Berry

1. David Skinner, "Awards & Honors: 2012 Jefferson Lecturer Wendell E. Berry Biography," National Endowment for the Humanities, www.neh.gov/about/awards/jefferson-lecture/wendell-e-berry-biography (accessed July 17, 2015).
2. Wendell Berry and Morris Allen Grubbs, *Conversations with Wendell Berry* (Jackson, MS: University Press of Mississippi, 2007), 51.

Chapter 2 An Adventure into Wonder—Hildegard of Bingen

1. Charles Moffat, "Hildegard of Bingen: The Biography of a Feminist Nun," *The Feminist eZine* (2002); www.feministezine.com/feminist/HildegardVonBingen-FeministNun.html.
2. Lexbook Online Dictionary; http://lexbook.net/en/viridity (accessed February 10, 2016).
3. Renate Craine, *Hildegard: Prophet of the Cosmic Christ* (New York: The Crossroad Publishing Company, 1997), 84.

Chapter 3 An Adventure into Anazement—Mary Oliver

1. From "Staying Alive," in *West Wind* (New York: Mariner Books, 1998).
2. Steven Ratiner, "Poet Mary Oliver: A Solitary Walk," *Christian Science Monitor*, December 9, 1992; www.csmonitor.com/1992/1209/09161.html.

Chapter 4 An Adventure into the
Wild—Clarissa Pinkola Estes

1. Dirk Johnson, "Conversations/Clarissa Pinkola Estes; A Message for All Women: Run Free and Wild Like the Wolf," *New York Times*, February 28, 1993; www.nytimes.com/1993/02/28/weekinreview/conversations-clarissa-pinkola-estes-message-for-all-women-run-free-wild-like.html.

Chapter 5 An Adventure into the Beautiful—John Muir

1. John Muir, *The Story of My Boyhood and Youth: My First Summer in the Sierra, the Mountains of California* (Des Moines, IA: Library of America, 1997), 34.
2. John Muir, *Travels in Alaska* (Cedar Lake, MI: ReadaClassic.com, 2012), 5.
3. I originally found this term in Jon Young, Evan McGown, and Ellen Haas, *Coyote's Guide to Connecting with Nature* (Shelton, WA: owLink Media, 2010).
4. Linnie Marsh Wolfe, ed., *John of the Mountains: The Unpublished Journals of John Muir* (Madison, WI: University of Wisconsin Press, 1979), 321.
5. Glenn Clark, *The Man Who Talks with the Flowers: The Intimate Life Story of Dr. George Washington Carver* (Eastford, CT: Martino Fine Books, 2011), 5.

Chapter 6 An Adventure into the Heart
of Things—Rainer Maria Rilke

1. Ralph Freedman, *Life of a Poet: Rainer Maria Rilke* (Evanston, IL: Northwestern University Press, 1998).
2. Rainer Maria Rilke, "Buddha in Glory," in *Ahead of All Parting: The Selected Poetry and Prose of Rainer Maria Rilke*, trans. Stephen Mitchell (New York: Modern Library, 1995).
3. Jeff A. Benner, "Hebrew Word Definitions," Ancient Hebrew Research Center; www.ancient-hebrew.org/vocabulary _definitions.html (accessed June 2, 2015).

Chapter 7 An Adventure into the Present—T.S. Eliot

1. Robert Sencourt, *T.S. Eliot: A Memoir* (London: Garnstone Limited, 1971), 18.

Chapter 8 An Adventure into Darkness—John O'Donohue

1. Krista Tippett, "Transcript for John O'Donohue—The Inner Landscape of Beauty," *On Being*, January 26, 2012; www.onbeing.org/program/inner-landscape-beauty/ transcript/1125.
2. John O'Donohue, *Anam Cara: A Book of Celtic Wisdom* (New York: Harper Perennial, 1998).
3. Ibid.
4. John O'Donohue, *To Bless the Space Between Us* (New York City: Doubleday, 2008), 198.

Chapter 9 An Adventure into Unseen Worlds—Joy Harjo

1. Joy Harjo, *Crazy Brave: A Memoir* (New York: W. W. Norton & Company, 2013), 28.
2. Ibid., 25.
3. Cassie Premo Steele, "Crazy Brave: An Interview with Joy Harjo and Review of Her New Memoir," *Literary Mama* (September 2012); www.literarymama.com/reviews/archives/ 2012/09/crazy-brave-an-interview-joy-h.html.

Chapter 10 An Adventure into the
Surprising—Flannery O'Connor

1. James Mackinnon, "Grace and Danger: A Flannery O'Connor Retrospective," *The Quietus* (August 31, 2014); http://the quietus.com/articles/16030-flannery-oconnor-fifty-years -anniversary-southern-gothic-true-detective.
2. Rosemary M. Magee, ed., *Conversations with Flannery O'Connor* (Jackson: University Press of Mississippi, 1987), 38.
3. Flannery O'Connor, *Mystery and Manners: Occasional Prose* (New York: Farrar, Straus and Giroux, 1969), 38.
4. Ibid., 34.

Chapter 11 An Adventure into Connectivity—Chief Seattle

1. Peter Stekel, "Who Was Chief Seattle and Did He Really Say, 'The Earth Does Not Belong to Man; Man Belongs to the Earth'?" *Wild West* magazine; www.peterstekel.com/PDF -HTML/ChiefSeattle.PDF (accessed January 24, 2016).
2. www.californiaindianeducation.org/famous_indian_chiefs/ chief_seattle (accessed February 10, 2016).

Chapter 12 An Adventure into the Liminal—Annie Dillard

1. Annie Dillard, *Pilgrim at Tinker Creek* (New York: Harper Perennial Modern Classics, 2007), 243.
2. Ibid., 61.
3. Annie Dillard, *The Writing Life* (New York: Harper Perennial, 1996), 79.

AVAILABLE FROM BETTER BOOKSTORES.
TRY YOUR BOOKSTORE FIRST.

Inspiration

The Golden Rule and the Games People Play
The Ultimate Strategy for a Meaning-Filled Life
By Rami Shapiro
A guidebook for living a meaning-filled life—using the strategies of game theory and the wisdom of the Golden Rule.
6 x 9, 176 pp, Quality PB, 978-1-59473-598-1 **$16.99**

Deepening Engagement
Essential Wisdom for Listening and Leading with Purpose, Meaning and Joy
By Diane M. Millis, PhD; Foreword by Rob Lehman
A toolkit for community building as well as a resource for personal growth and small group enrichment.
5 x 7¼, 176 pp, Quality PB, 978-1-59473-584-4 **$14.99**

The Rebirthing of God
Christianity's Struggle for New Beginnings
By John Philip Newell
Drawing on modern prophets from East and West, and using the holy island of Iona as an icon of new beginnings, Newell dares us to imagine a new birth from deep within Christianity, a fresh stirring of the Spirit.
6 x 9, 160 pp, HC, 978-1-59473-542-4 **$19.99**

Finding God Beyond Religion: A Guide for Skeptics, Agnostics & Unorthodox Believers Inside & Outside the Church
By Tom Stella; Foreword by The Rev. Canon Marianne Wells Borg
Reinterprets traditional religious teachings central to the Christian faith for people who have outgrown the beliefs and devotional practices that once made sense to them. 6 x 9, 160 pp, Quality PB, 978-1-59473-485-4 **$16.99**

Fully Awake and Truly Alive: Spiritual Practices to Nurture Your Soul
By Rev. Jane E. Vennard; Foreword by Rami Shapiro
Illustrates the joys and frustrations of spiritual practice across religious traditions; provides exercises and meditations to help you become more fully alive.
6 x 9, 208 pp, Quality PB, 978-1-59473-473-1 **$16.99**

Perennial Wisdom for the Spiritually Independent
Sacred Teachings—Annotated & Explained
Annotation by Rami Shapiro; Foreword by Richard Rohr
Weaves sacred texts and teachings from the world's major religions into a coherent exploration of the five core questions at the heart of every religion's search.
5½ x 8½, 336 pp, Quality PB, 978-1-59473-515-8 **$16.99**

Journeys of Simplicity: Traveling Light with Thomas Merton, Bashō, Edward Abbey, Annie Dillard & Others *By Philip Harnden*
5 x 7¼, 144 pp, Quality PB, 978-1-59473-181-5 **$12.99**

Saving Civility: 52 Ways to Tame Rude, Crude & Attitude for a Polite Planet
By Sara Hacala 6 x 9, 240 pp, Quality PB, 978-1-59473-314-7 **$16.99**

Spiritually Healthy Divorce: Navigating Disruption with Insight & Hope
By Carolyne Call 6 x 9, 224 pp, Quality PB, 978-1-59473-288-1 **$16.99**

Or phone, fax, mail or email to: SKYLIGHT PATHS Publishing
Sunset Farm Offices, Route 4 • P.O. Box 237 • Woodstock, Vermont 05091
Tel: (802) 457-4000 • Fax: (802) 457-4004 • www.skylightpaths.com
Credit card orders: (800) 962-4544 (8:30AM–5:30PM EST Monday–Friday)
Generous discounts on quantity orders. SATISFACTION GUARANTEED. Prices subject to change.

Retirement and Later-Life Spirituality

Caresharing
A Reciprocal Approach to Caregiving and Care Receiving in the Complexities of Aging, Illness or Disability
By Marty Richards

Shows how to move from independent to *inter*dependent caregiving, so that the "cared for" and the "carer" share a deep sense of connection.

6 x 9, 256 pp, Quality PB, 978-1-59473-286-7 **$16.99**; HC, 978-1-59473-247-8 **$24.99**

How Did I Get to Be 70 When I'm 35 Inside?
Spiritual Surprises of Later Life
By Linda Douty

Encourages you to focus on the inner changes of aging to help you greet your later years as the grand adventure they can be.

6 x 9, 208 pp, Quality PB, 978-1-59473-297-3 **$16.99**

Soul Fire
Accessing Your Creativity
By Thomas Ryan, CSP

This inspiring guide shows you how to cultivate your creative spirit, particularly in the second half of life, as a way to encourage personal growth, enrich your spiritual life and deepen your communion with God.

6 x 9, 160 pp, Quality PB, 978-1-59473-243-0 **$16.99**

Restoring Life's Missing Pieces
The Spiritual Power of Remembering & Reuniting with People, Places, Things & Self
By Caren Goldman; Foreword by Dr. Nancy Copeland-Payton

Delve deeply into ways that your body, mind and spirit answer the Spirit of Re-union's calls to reconnect with people, places, things and self. A powerful and thought-provoking look at "reunions" of all kinds as roads to remembering the missing pieces of our stories, psyches and souls.

6 x 9, 208 pp, Quality PB, 978-1-59473-295-9 **$16.99**

Creative Aging
Rethinking Retirement and Non-Retirement in a Changing World
By Marjory Zoet Bankson

Explores the spiritual dimensions of retirement and aging and offers creative ways for you to share your gifts and experience, particularly when retirement leaves you questioning who you are when you are no longer defined by your career.

6 x 9, 160 pp, Quality PB, 978-1-59473-281-2 **$16.99**

Creating a Spiritual Retirement
A Guide to the Unseen Possibilities in Our Lives
By Molly Srode

Retirement can be an opportunity to refocus on your soul and deepen the presence of spirit in your life. With fresh spiritual reflections and questions to help you explore this new phase.

6 x 9, 208 pp, b/w photos, Quality PB, 978-1-59473-050-4 **$14.99**

Keeping Spiritual Balance as We Grow Older
More than 65 Creative Ways to Use Purpose, Prayer, and the Power of Spirit to Build a Meaningful Retirement
By Molly and Bernie Srode

As we face new demands on our bodies, it's easy to focus on the physical and forget about the transformations in our spiritual selves. This book is brimming with creative, practical ideas to add purpose and spirit to a meaningful retirement.

8 x 8, 224 pp, Quality PB, 978-1-59473-042-9 **$16.99**

Spirituality

Mere Spirituality
The Spiritual Life According to Henri Nouwen
By Wil Hernandez, PhD, Obl. OSB; Foreword by Ronald Rolheiser
This introduction to Nouwen's spiritual thought distills key insights on the realm of the spiritual life into one concise and compelling overview of his spirituality of the heart.
6 x 9, 160 pp, Quality PB, 978-1-59473-586-8 **$16.99**

The Forgiveness Handbook
Spiritual Wisdom and Practice for the Journey to Freedom, Healing and Peace
Created by the Editors at SkyLight Paths; Introduction by The Rev. Canon Marianne Wells Borg
Offers inspiration, encouragement and spiritual practice from across faith traditions for all who seek hope, wholeness and the freedom that comes from true forgiveness.
6 x 9, 256 pp, Quality PB, 978-1-59473-577-6 **$18.99**

Like a Child
Restoring the Awe, Wonder, Joy and Resiliency of the Human Spirit
By Rev. Timothy J. Mooney
By breaking free from our misperceptions about what it means to be an adult, we can reshape our world and become harbingers of grace. This unique spiritual resource explores Jesus's counsel to become like children in order to enter the kingdom of God. 6 x 9, 160 pp, Quality PB, 978-1-59473-543-1 **$16.99**

The Passionate Jesus: What We Can Learn from Jesus about Love, Fear, Grief, Joy and Living Authentically
By The Rev. Peter Wallace
Reveals Jesus as a passionate figure who was involved, present, connected, honest and direct with others and encourages you to build personal authenticity in every area of your own life. 6 x 9, 208 pp, Quality PB, 978-1-59473-393-2 **$18.99**

Gathering at God's Table: The Meaning of Mission in the Feast of Faith
By Katharine Jefferts Schori
A profound reminder of our role in the larger frame of God's dream for a restored and reconciled world. 6 x 9, 256 pp, HC, 978-1-59473-316-1 **$21.99**

The Heartbeat of God: Finding the Sacred in the Middle of Everything
By Katharine Jefferts Schori; Foreword by Joan Chittister, OSB
Explores our connections to other people, to other nations and with the environment through the lens of faith.
6 x 9, 240 pp, HC, 978-1-59473-292-8 **$21.99**; Quality PB, 978-1-59473-589-9 **$16.99**

Laugh Your Way to Grace: Reclaiming the Spiritual Power of Humor
By Rev. Susan Sparks
A powerful, humorous case for laughter as a spiritual, healing path.
6 x 9, 176 pp, Quality PB, 978-1-59473-280-5 **$16.99**

Claiming Earth as Common Ground: The Ecological Crisis through the Lens of Faith
By Andrea Cohen-Kiener; Foreword by Rev. Sally Bingham
6 x 9, 192 pp, Quality PB, 978-1-59473-261-4 **$16.99**

Living into Hope: A Call to Spiritual Action for Such a Time as This
By Rev. Dr. Joan Brown Campbell; Foreword by Karen Armstrong
6 x 9, 208 pp, Quality PB, 978-1-59473-436-6 **$18.99**;
HC, 978-1-59473-283-6 **$21.99**

Renewal in the Wilderness
A Spiritual Guide to Connecting with God in the Natural World
By John Lionberger
6 x 9, 176 pp, b/w photos, Quality PB, 978-1-59473-219-5 **$16.99**

A Walk with Four Spiritual Guides: Krishna, Buddha, Jesus, and Ramakrishna
By Andrew Harvey
5½ x 8½, 192 pp, b/w photos & illus., Quality PB, 978-1-59473-138-9 **$18.99**

Sacred Texts—SkyLight Illuminations Series

Offers today's spiritual seeker an enjoyable entry into the great classic texts of the world's spiritual traditions. Each classic is presented in an accessible translation, with facing pages of guided commentary from experts, giving you the keys you need to understand the history, context and meaning of the text.

CHRISTIANITY

The Book of Common Prayer: A Spiritual Treasure Chest—Selections Annotated & Explained
Annotation by The Rev. Canon C. K. Robertson, PhD; Foreword by The Most Rev. Katharine Jefferts Schori; Preface by Archbishop Desmond Tutu
Makes available the riches of this spiritual treasure chest for all who are interested in deepening their life of prayer, building stronger relationships and making a difference in their world. 5½ x 8½, 208 pp, Quality PB, 978-1-59473-524-0 **$16.99**

Celtic Christian Spirituality: Essential Writings—Annotated & Explained
Annotation by Mary C. Earle; Foreword by John Philip Newell
Explores how the writings of this lively tradition embody the gospel.
5½ x 8½, 176 pp, Quality PB, 978-1-59473-302-4 **$16.99**

Desert Fathers and Mothers: Early Christian Wisdom Sayings—Annotated & Explained *Annotation by Christine Valters Paintner, PhD*
Opens up wisdom of the desert fathers and mothers for readers with no previous knowledge of Western monasticism and early Christianity.
5½ x 8½, 192 pp, Quality PB, 978-1-59473-373-4 **$16.99**

The End of Days: Essential Selections from Apocalyptic Texts—Annotated & Explained *Annotation by Robert G. Clouse, PhD*
Helps you understand the complex Christian visions of the end of the world.
5½ x 8½, 224 pp, Quality PB, 978-1-59473-170-9 **$16.99**

The Hidden Gospel of Matthew: Annotated & Explained
Translation & Annotation by Ron Miller
Discover the words and events that have the strongest connection to the historical Jesus.
5½ x 8½, 272 pp, Quality PB, 978-1-59473-038-2 **$16.99**

The Imitation of Christ: Selections Annotated & Explained
Annotation by Paul Wesley Chilcote, PhD; By Thomas à Kempis
Adapted from John Wesley's The Christian's Pattern
Let Jesus's example of holiness, humility and purity of heart be a companion on your own spiritual journey. 5½ x 8½, 224 pp, Quality PB, 978-1-59473-434-2 **$16.99**

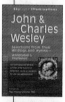

The Infancy Gospels of Jesus: Apocryphal Tales from the Childhoods of Mary and Jesus—Annotated & Explained
Translation & Annotation by Stevan Davies; Foreword by A. Edward Siecienski, PhD
A startling presentation of the early lives of Mary, Jesus and other biblical figures that will amuse and surprise you. 5½ x 8½, 176 pp, Quality PB, 978-1-59473-258-4 **$16.99**

John & Charles Wesley: Selections from Their Writings and Hymns—Annotated & Explained *Annotation by Paul W. Chilcote, PhD*
A unique presentation of the writings of these two inspiring brothers brings together some of the most essential material from their large corpus of work.
5½ x 8½, 288 pp, Quality PB, 978-1-59473-309-3 **$16.99**

Julian of Norwich: Selections from *Revelations of Divine Love*—Annotated & Explained *Annotation by Mary C. Earle; Foreword by Roberta C. Bondi*
Addresses topics including the infinite nature of God, the life of prayer, God's suffering with us, the eternal and undying life of the soul, the motherhood of Jesus and the motherhood of God and more.
5½ x 8½, 224 pp, Quality PB, 978-1-59473-513-4 **$16.99**

Sacred Texts—continued

CHRISTIANITY—continued

The Lost Sayings of Jesus: Teachings from Ancient Christian, Jewish, Gnostic and Islamic Sources—Annotated & Explained
Translation & Annotation by Andrew Phillip Smith; Foreword by Stephan A. Hoeller
Depicts Jesus as a Wisdom teacher who speaks to people of all faiths as a mystic and spiritual master. 5½ x 8½, 240 pp, Quality PB, 978-1-59473-172-3 **$16.99**

Philokalia: The Eastern Christian Spiritual Texts—Selections
Annotated & Explained *Annotation by Allyne Smith; Translation by G. E. H. Palmer, Phillip Sherrard and Bishop Kallistos Ware* The first approachable introduction to the wisdom of the Philokalia. 5½ x 8½, 240 pp, Quality PB, 978-1-59473-103-7 **$18.99**

The Sacred Writings of Paul: Selections Annotated & Explained
Translation & Annotation by Ron Miller Leads you into the exciting immediacy of Paul's teachings. 5½ x 8½, 224 pp, Quality PB, 978-1-59473-213-3 **$16.99**

Saint Augustine of Hippo: Selections from *Confessions* and Other Essential Writings—Annotated & Explained
Annotation by Joseph T. Kelley, PhD; Translation by the Augustinian Heritage Institute
Provides insight into the mind and heart of this foundational Christian figure.
5½ x 8½, 272 pp, Quality PB, 978-1-59473-282-9 **$18.99**

Saint Ignatius Loyola—The Spiritual Writings: Selections
Annotated & Explained *Annotation by Mark Mossa, SJ* Focuses on the practical mysticism of Ignatius of Loyola. 5½ x 8½, 288 pp, Quality PB, 978-1-59473-301-7 **$18.99**

Sex Texts from the Bible: Selections Annotated & Explained
Translation & Annotation by Teresa J. Hornsby; Foreword by Amy-Jill Levine
Demystifies the Bible's ideas on gender roles, marriage, sexual orientation, virginity, lust and sexual pleasure. 5½ x 8½, 208 pp, Quality PB, 978-1-59473-217-1 **$16.99**

Spiritual Writings on Mary: Annotated & Explained
Annotation by Mary Ford-Grabowsky; Foreword by Andrew Harvey
Examines the role of Mary, the mother of Jesus, as a source of inspiration in history and in life today. 5½ x 8½, 272 pp, Quality PB, 978-1-59473-001-6 **$16.99**

The Way of a Pilgrim: The Jesus Prayer Journey—Annotated & Explained
Translation & Annotation by Gleb Pokrovsky; Foreword by Andrew Harvey A classic of Russian Orthodox spirituality. 5½ x 8½, 160 pp, Illus., Quality PB, 978-1-893361-31-7 **$15.99**

GNOSTICISM

Gnostic Writings on the Soul: Annotated & Explained
Translation & Annotation by Andrew Phillip Smith; Foreword by Stephan A. Hoeller
Reveals the inspiring ways your soul can remember and return to its unique, divine purpose. 5½ x 8½, 144 pp, Quality PB, 978-1-59473-220-1 **$16.99**

The Gospel of Philip: Annotated & Explained
Translation & Annotation by Andrew Phillip Smith; Foreword by Stevan Davies
Reveals otherwise unrecorded sayings of Jesus and fragments of Gnostic mythology.
5½ x 8½, 160 pp, Quality PB, 978-1-59473-111-2 **$16.99**

The Gospel of Thomas: Annotated & Explained
Translation & Annotation by Stevan Davies; Foreword by Andrew Harvey
Sheds new light on the origins of Christianity and portrays Jesus as a wisdom-loving sage.
5½ x 8½, 192 pp, Quality PB, 978-1-893361-45-4 **$16.99**

The Secret Book of John: The Gnostic Gospel—Annotated & Explained
Translation & Annotation by Stevan Davies The most significant and influential text of the ancient Gnostic religion. 5½ x 8½, 208 pp, Quality PB, 978-1-59473-082-5 **$18.99**

See Inspiration for *Perennial Wisdom for the Spiritually Independent: Sacred Teachings—Annotated & Explained*

Sacred Texts—continued

JUDAISM

The Book of Job: Annotated & Explained
Translation and Annotation by Donald Kraus; Foreword by Dr. Marc Brettler
Clarifies for today's readers what Job is, how to overcome difficulties in the text, and what it may mean for us. 5½ x 8½, 256 pp, Quality PB, 978-1-59473-389-5 **$16.99**

The Divine Feminine in Biblical Wisdom Literature
Selections Annotated & Explained
Translation & Annotation by Rabbi Rami Shapiro; Foreword by Rev. Cynthia Bourgeault, PhD
Uses the Hebrew Bible and Wisdom literature to explain Sophia's way of wisdom and illustrate Her creative energy. 5½ x 8½, 240 pp, Quality PB, 978-1-59473-109-9 **$18.99**

Ecclesiastes: Annotated & Explained
Translation & Annotation by Rabbi Rami Shapiro; Foreword by Rev. Barbara Cawthorne Crafton
A timeless teaching on living well amid uncertainty and insecurity.
5½ x 8½, 160 pp, Quality PB, 978-1-59473-287-4 **$16.99**

Embracing the Divine Feminine: Finding God through the Ecstasy of Physical Love—The Song of Songs Annotated & Explained
Translation & Annotation by Rabbi Rami Shapiro; Foreword by Rev. Cynthia Bourgeault, PhD
Restores the Song of Songs' eroticism and interprets it as a celebration of the love between the Divine Feminine and the contemporary spiritual seeker.
5½ x 8½, 176 pp, Quality PB, 978-1-59473-575-2 **$16.99**

Ethics of the Sages: Pirke Avot—Annotated & Explained
Translation & Annotation by Rabbi Rami Shapiro Clarifies the ethical teachings of the early Rabbis. 5½ x 8½, 192 pp, Quality PB, 978-1-59473-207-2 **$16.99**

Hasidic Tales: Annotated & Explained
Translation & Annotation by Rabbi Rami Shapiro; Foreword by Andrew Harvey
Introduces the legendary tales of the impassioned Hasidic rabbis, presenting them as stories rather than as parables. 5½ x 8½, 240 pp, Quality PB, 978-1-893361-86-7 **$18.99**

The Hebrew Prophets: Selections Annotated & Explained
Translation & Annotation by Rabbi Rami Shapiro; Foreword by Rabbi Zalman M. Schachter-Shalomi (z"l)
Makes the wisdom of these timeless teachers available to readers with no previous knowledge of the prophets. 5½ x 8½, 224 pp, Quality PB, 978-1-59473-037-5 **$16.99**

Maimonides—Essential Teachings on Jewish Faith & Ethics
The Book of Knowledge & the Thirteen Principles of Faith—Annotated & Explained
Translation and Annotation by Rabbi Marc D. Angel, PhD
Opens up for us Maimonides's views on the nature of God, providence, prophecy, free will, human nature, repentance and more.
5½ x 8½, 224 pp, Quality PB, 978-1-59473-311-6 **$18.99**

Proverbs: Annotated & Explained
Translation and Annotation by Rabbi Rami Shapiro
Demonstrates how these complex poetic forms are actually straightforward instructions to live simply, without rationalizations and excuses.
5½ x 8½, 288 pp, Quality PB, 978-1-59473-310-9 **$16.99**

Tanya, the Masterpiece of Hasidic Wisdom
Selections Annotated & Explained *Translation & Annotation by Rabbi Rami Shapiro*
Foreword by Rabbi Zalman M. Schachter-Shalomi (z"l)
Clarifies one of the most powerful and potentially transformative books of Jewish wisdom. 5½ x 8½, 240 pp, Quality PB, 978-1-59473-275-1 **$18.99**

Zohar: Annotated & Explained
Translation & Annotation by Daniel C. Matt; Foreword by Andrew Harvey The canonical text of Jewish mystical tradition. 5½ x 8½, 176 pp, Quality PB, 978-1-893361-51-5 **$18.99**

See Inspiration for *Perennial Wisdom for the Spiritually Independent: Sacred Teachings—Annotated & Explained*

Sacred Texts—continued

ISLAM

Ghazali on the Principles of Islamic Spirituality
Selections from *The Forty Foundations of Religion*—Annotated & Explained
Translation & Annotation by Aaron Spevack, PhD; Foreword by M. Fethullah Gülen
Makes the core message of this influential spiritual master relevant to anyone seeking a balanced understanding of Islam.
5½ x 8½, 336 pp, Quality PB, 978-1-59473-284-3 **$18.99**

The Qur'an and Sayings of Prophet Muhammad
Selections Annotated & Explained
Annotation by Sohaib N. Sultan; Translation by Yusuf Ali, Revised by Sohaib N. Sultan
Foreword by Jane I. Smith
Presents the foundational wisdom of Islam in an easy-to-use format.
5½ x 8½, 256 pp, Quality PB, 978-1-59473-222-5 **$16.99**

Rumi and Islam: Selections from His Stories, Poems, and Discourses—
Annotated & Explained *Translation & Annotation by Ibrahim Gamard*
Focuses on Rumi's place within the Sufi tradition of Islam, providing insight into the mystical side of the religion. 5½ x 8½, 240 pp, Quality PB, 978-1-59473-002-3 **$18.99**

See Inspiration for *Perennial Wisdom for the Spiritually Independent: Sacred Teachings—Annotated & Explained*

EASTERN RELIGIONS

The Art of War—Spirituality for Conflict: Annotated & Explained
By Sun Tzu; Annotation by Thomas Huynh; Translation by Thomas Huynh and the Editors at Sonshi.com; Foreword by Marc Benioff; Preface by Thomas Cleary
Highlights principles that encourage a perceptive and spiritual approach to conflict.
5½ x 8½, 256 pp, Quality PB, 978-1-59473-244-7 **$16.99**

Bhagavad Gita: Annotated & Explained
Translation by Shri Purohit Swami; Annotation by Kendra Crossen Burroughs
Foreword by Andrew Harvey Presents the classic text's teachings—with no previous knowledge of Hinduism required. 5½ x 8½, 192 pp, Quality PB, 978-1-893361-28-7 **$18.99**

Chuang-tzu: The Tao of Perfect Happiness—Selections Annotated & Explained
Translation & Annotation by Livia Kohn, PhD
Presents Taoism's central message of reverence for the "Way" of the natural world.
5½ x 8½, 240 pp, Quality PB, 978-1-59473-296-6 **$16.99**

Confucius, the *Analects*: The Path of the Sage—Selections Annotated
& Explained *Annotation by Rodney L. Taylor, PhD; Translation by James Legge,*
Revised by Rodney L. Taylor, PhD Explores the ethical and spiritual meaning behind the Confucian way of learning and self-cultivation.
5½ x 8½, 192 pp, Quality PB, 978-1-59473-306-2 **$16.99**

Dhammapada: Annotated & Explained
Translation by Max Müller, Revised by Jack Maguire; Annotation by Jack Maguire
Foreword by Andrew Harvey Contains all of Buddhism's key teachings, plus commentary that explains all the names, terms and references.
5½ x 8½, 160 pp, b/w photos, Quality PB, 978-1-893361-42-3 **$14.95**

Selections from the Gospel of Sri Ramakrishna: Annotated & Explained
Translation by Swami Nikhilananda; Annotation by Kendra Crossen Burroughs
Foreword by Andrew Harvey Introduces the fascinating world of the Indian mystic and the universal appeal of his message. 5½ x 8½, 240 pp, b/w photos, Quality PB, 978-1-893361-46-1 **$16.95**

Tao Te Ching: Annotated & Explained
Translation & Annotation by Derek Lin; Foreword by Lama Surya Das
Introduces an Eastern classic in an accessible, poetic and completely original way.
5½ x 8½, 208 pp, Quality PB, 978-1-59473-204-1 **$16.99**

Spirituality / Animal Companions

Blessing the Animals
Prayers and Ceremonies to Celebrate God's Creatures, Wild and Tame
Edited and with Introductions by Lynn L. Caruso
5 x 7¼, 256 pp, Quality PB, 978-1-59473-253-9 **$15.99**; HC, 978-1-59473-145-7 **$19.99**

Remembering My Pet
A Kid's Own Spiritual Workbook for When a Pet Dies
By Nechama Liss-Levinson, PhD, and Rev. Molly Phinney Baskette, MDiv
Foreword by Lynn L. Caruso
8 x 10, 48 pp, 2-color text, HC, 978-1-59473-221-8 **$16.99**

What Animals Can Teach Us about Spirituality
Inspiring Lessons from Wild and Tame Creatures
By Diana L. Guerrero 6 x 9, 176 pp, Quality PB, 978-1-893361-84-3 **$18.99**

Spirituality & Crafts

The Advent of God's Word
Listening for the Power of the Divine Whisper—A Daily Retreat &
Devotional *By Rev. Dr. Brenda K. Buckwell, Obl. OSB*
For those who find themselves struggling with no time for prayer during the busy Advent season. Step-by-step creative exercises help you celebrate the birth of Jesus and enter the new calendar year with a personal pictorial journal of the season. 6 x 9, 208 pp, Quality PB, 978-1-59473-576-9 **$16.99**

Beading—The Creative Spirit
Finding Your Sacred Center through the Art of Beadwork
By Rev. Wendy Ellsworth Invites you on a spiritual pilgrimage into the kaleidoscope world of glass and color. 7 x 9, 240 pp, 8-page color insert, 40+ b/w photos and 40 diagrams; Quality PB, 978-1-59473-267-6 **$18.99**

Contemplative Crochet
A Hands-On Guide for Interlocking Faith and Craft
By Cindy Crandall-Frazier; Foreword by Linda Skolnik
Illuminates the spiritual lessons you can learn through crocheting.
7 x 9, 208 pp, b/w photos, Quality PB, 978-1-59473-238-6 **$16.99**

The Knitting Way
A Guide to Spiritual Self-Discovery
By Linda Skolnik and Janice MacDaniels
Examines how you can explore and strengthen your spiritual life through knitting.
7 x 9, 240 pp, b/w photos, Quality PB, 978-1-59473-079-5 **$16.99**

The Painting Path
Embodying Spiritual Discovery through Yoga, Brush and Color
By Linda Novick; Foreword by Richard Segalman
Explores the divine connection you can experience through art.
7 x 9, 208 pp, 8-page color insert, plus b/w photos, Quality PB, 978-1-59473-226-3 **$18.99**

The Soulwork of Clay
A Hands-On Approach to Spirituality
By Marjory Zoet Bankson; Photos by Peter Bankson
Takes you through the seven-step process of making clay into a pot, drawing parallels at each stage to the process of spiritual growth.
7 x 9, 192 pp, b/w photos, Quality PB, 978-1-59473-249-2 **$16.99**

The Quilting Path: A Guide to Spiritual Discovery through Fabric, Thread and Kabbalah
By Louise Silk 7 x 9, 192 pp, b/w photos and illus., Quality PB, 978-1-59473-206-5 **$16.99**

The Scrapbooking Journey: A Hands-On Guide to Spiritual Discovery
By Cory Richardson-Lauve; Foreword by Stacy Julian
7 x 9, 176 pp, 8-page color insert, plus b/w photos, Quality PB, 978-1-59473-216-4 **$18.99**

Spiritual Practice—The Sacred Art of Living Series

Teaching—The Sacred Art: The Joy of Opening Minds & Hearts
By Rev. Jane E. Vennard Explores the elements that make teaching a sacred art, recognizing it as a call to service rather than a job, and a vocation rather than a profession. 5½ x 8½, 160 pp, Quality PB, 978-1-59473-585-1 **$16.99**

Conversation—The Sacred Art: Practicing Presence in an Age of Distraction
By Diane M. Millis, PhD; Foreword by Rev. Tilden Edwards, PhD
5½ x 8½, 192 pp, Quality PB, 978-1-59473-474-8 **$16.99**

Dance—The Sacred Art: The Joy of Movement as a Spiritual Practice
By Cynthia Winton-Henry 5½ x 8½, 224 pp, Quality PB, 978-1-59473-268-3 **$16.99**

Dreaming—The Sacred Art: Incubating, Navigating & Interpreting Sacred Dreams for Spiritual & Personal Growth *By Lori Joan Swick, PhD*
5½ x 8½, 224 pp, Quality PB, 978-1-59473-544-8 **$16.99**

Fly-Fishing—The Sacred Art: Casting a Fly as a Spiritual Practice
By Rabbi Eric Eisenkramer and Rev. Michael Attas, MD; Foreword by Chris Wood, CEO, Trout Unlimited; Preface by Lori Simon, executive director, Casting for Recovery
5½ x 8½, 160 pp, Quality PB, 978-1-59473-299-7 **$16.99**

Giving—The Sacred Art: Creating a Lifestyle of Generosity
By Lauren Tyler Wright 5½ x 8½, 208 pp, Quality PB, 978-1-59473-224-9 **$16.99**

Haiku—The Sacred Art: A Spiritual Practice in Three Lines
By Margaret D. McGee 5½ x 8½, 192 pp, Quality PB, 978-1-59473-269-0 **$16.99**

Hospitality—The Sacred Art: Discovering the Hidden Spiritual Power of Invitation and Welcome *By Rev. Nanette Sawyer; Foreword by Rev. Dirk Ficca*
5½ x 8½, 208 pp, Quality PB, 978-1-59473-228-7 **$16.99**

Labyrinths from the Outside In, 2nd Edition
Walking to Spiritual Insight—A Beginner's Guide *By Rev. Dr. Donna Schaper and Rev. Dr. Carole Ann Camp* 6 x 9, 208 pp, b/w illus. and photos, Quality PB, 978-1-59473-486-1 **$16.99**

***Lectio Divina*—The Sacred Art**
Transforming Words & Images into Heart-Centered Prayer
By Christine Valters Paintner, PhD 5½ x 8½, 240 pp, Quality PB, 978-1-59473-300-0 **$16.99**

Pilgrimage—The Sacred Art: Journey to the Center of the Heart
By Dr. Sheryl A. Kujawa-Holbrook 5½ x 8½, 240 pp, Quality PB, 978-1-59473-472-4 **$16.99**

Practicing the Sacred Art of Listening
A Guide to Enrich Your Relationships and Kindle Your Spiritual Life
By Kay Lindahl 8 x 8, 176 pp, Quality PB, 978-1-893361-85-0 **$18.99**

Recovery—The Sacred Art: The Twelve Steps as Spiritual Practice *By Rami Shapiro*
Foreword by Joan Borysenko, PhD 5½ x 8½, 240 pp, Quality PB, 978-1-59473-259-1 **$16.99**

Running—The Sacred Art: Preparing to Practice *By Dr. Warren A. Kay*
Foreword by Kristin Armstrong 5½ x 8½, 160 pp, Quality PB, 978-1-59473-227-0 **$16.99**

The Sacred Art of Chant: Preparing to Practice
By Ana Hernández 5½ x 8½, 192 pp, Quality PB, 978-1-59473-036-8 **$16.99**

The Sacred Art of Fasting: Preparing to Practice
By Thomas Ryan, CSP 5½ x 8½, 192 pp, Quality PB, 978-1-59473-078-8 **$15.99**

The Sacred Art of Forgiveness: Forgiving Ourselves and Others through God's Grace
By Marcia Ford 8 x 8, 176 pp, Quality PB, 978-1-59473-175-4 **$18.99**

The Sacred Art of Listening: Forty Reflections for Cultivating a Spiritual Practice
By Kay Lindahl; Illus. by Amy Schnapper 8 x 8, 160 pp, b/w illus., Quality PB, 978-1-893361-44-7 **$16.99**

The Sacred Art of Lovingkindness: Preparing to Practice
By Rabbi Rami Shapiro; Foreword by Marcia Ford 5½ x 8½, 176 pp, Quality PB, 978-1-59473-151-8 **$16.99**

Spiritual Adventures in the Snow: Skiing & Snowboarding as Renewal for Your Soul
By Dr. Marcia McFee and Rev. Karen Foster; Foreword by Paul Arthur
5½ x 8½, 208 pp, Quality PB, 978-1-59473-270-6 **$16.99**

Thanking & Blessing—The Sacred Art: Spiritual Vitality through Gratefulness
By Jay Marshall, PhD; Foreword by Philip Gulley 5½ x 8½, 176 pp, Quality PB, 978-1-59473-231-7 **$16.99**

Writing—The Sacred Art: Beyond the Page to Spiritual Practice
By Rami Shapiro and Aaron Shapiro 5½ x 8½, 192 pp, Quality PB, 978-1-59473-372-7 **$16.99**

Children's Spiritual Biography

MULTICULTURAL, NONDENOMINATIONAL, NONSECTARIAN

Ten Amazing People
And How They Changed the World
By Maura D. Shaw; Foreword by Dr. Robert Coles
Full-color illus. by Stephen Marchesi

For ages 7 & up

Shows kids that spiritual people can have an exciting impact on the world around them. Kids will delight in reading about these amazing people and what they accomplished through their words and actions.

Black Elk • Dorothy Day • Malcolm X • Mahatma Gandhi • Martin Luther King, Jr. • Mother Teresa • Janusz Korczak • Desmond Tutu • Thich Nhat Hanh • Albert Schweitzer

"Best Juvenile/Young Adult Non-Fiction Book of the Year."
—*Independent Publisher*

"Will inspire adults and children alike."
—*Globe and Mail* (Toronto)

8½ x 11, 48 pp, Full-color illus., HC, 978-1-893361-47-8 **$18.99** For ages 7 & up

Spiritual Biographies for Young People
For Ages 7 & Up

By Maura D. Shaw; Illus. by Stephen Marchesi 6¾ x 8¾, 32 pp, Full-color and b/w illus., HC

Black Elk: Native American Man of Spirit
Through historically accurate illustrations and photos, inspiring age-appropriate activities and Black Elk's own words, this colorful biography introduces children to a remarkable person who ensured that the traditions and beliefs of his people would not be forgotten.
978-1-59473-043-6 **$12.99**

Dorothy Day: A Catholic Life of Action
Introduces children to one of the most inspiring women of the twentieth century, a down-to-earth spiritual leader who saw the presence of God in every person she met. Includes practical activities, a timeline and a list of important words to know.
978-1-59473-011-5 **$12.99**

Gandhi: India's Great Soul
The only biography of Gandhi that balances a simple text with illustrations, photos and activities that encourage children and adults to talk about how to make changes happen without violence. Introduces children to important concepts of freedom, equality and justice among people of all backgrounds and religions.
978-1-893361-91-1 **$12.95**

Thich Nhat Hanh: Buddhism in Action
Warm illustrations, photos, age-appropriate activities and Thich Nhat Hanh's own poems introduce a great man to children in a way they can understand and enjoy. Includes a list of important Buddhist words to know.
978-1-893361-87-4 **$12.95**

Spiritual Poetry—The Mystic Poets

Experience these mystic poets as you never have before. Each beautiful, compact book includes a brief introduction to the poet's time and place, a summary of the major themes of the poet's mysticism and religious tradition, essential selections from the poet's most important works, and an appreciative preface by a contemporary spiritual writer.

Hafiz
The Mystic Poets
Translated and with Notes by Gertrude Bell
Preface by Ibrahim Gamard
Hafiz is known throughout the world as Persia's greatest poet, with sales of his poems in Iran today only surpassed by those of the Qur'an itself. His probing and joyful verse speaks to people from all backgrounds who long to taste and feel divine love and experience harmony with all living things.
5 x 7¼, 144 pp, HC, 978-1-59473-009-2 **$16.99**

Hopkins
The Mystic Poets
Preface by Rev. Thomas Ryan, CSP
Gerard Manley Hopkins, Christian mystical poet, is beloved for his use of fresh language and startling metaphors to describe the world around him. Although his verse is lovely, beneath the surface lies a searching soul, wrestling with and yearning for God.
5 x 7¼, 112 pp, HC, 978-1-59473-010-8 **$16.99**

Tagore
The Mystic Poets
Preface by Swami Adiswarananda
Rabindranath Tagore is often considered the Shakespeare of modern India. A great mystic, Tagore was the teacher of W. B. Yeats and Robert Frost, the close friend of Albert Einstein and Mahatma Gandhi, and the winner of the Nobel Prize for Literature. This beautiful sampling of Tagore's two most important works, *The Gardener* and *Gitanjali,* offers a glimpse into his spiritual vision that has inspired people around the world.
5 x 7¼, 144 pp, HC, 978-1-59473-008-5 **$16.99**

Whitman
The Mystic Poets
Preface by Gary David Comstock
Walt Whitman was the most innovative and influential poet of the nineteenth century. This beautiful sampling of Whitman's most important poetry from *Leaves of Grass,* and selections from his prose writings, offers a glimpse into the spiritual side of his most radical themes—love for country, love for others and love of self.
5 x 7¼, 192 pp, HC, 978-1-59473-041-2 **$16.99**

Prayer / Meditation

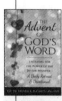

The Advent of God's Word
Listening for the Power of the Divine Whisper—A Daily Retreat & Devotional
By Rev. Dr. Brenda K. Buckwell, Obl. OSB
For those who find themselves struggling with no time for prayer during the busy Advent season. Step-by-step creative exercises help you celebrate the birth of Jesus.
6 x 9, 208 pp, Quality PB, 978-1-59473-576-9 **$16.99**

Calling on God
Inclusive Christian Prayers for Three Years of Sundays
By Peter Bankson and Deborah Sokolove
Prayers for today's world, vividly written for Christians who long for a way to talk to and about God that feels fresh yet still connected to tradition.
6 x 9, 400 pp, Quality PB, 978-1-59473-568-4 **$18.99**
The Worship Leader's Guide to Calling on God
8½ x 11, 20 pp, PB, 978-1-59473-591-2 **$9.99**

Openings, 2nd Edition
A Daybook of Saints, Sages, Psalms and Prayer Practices
By Rev. Larry J. Peacock
For anyone hungry for a richer prayer life, this prayer book offers daily inspiration to help you move closer to God. Draws on a wide variety of resources—lives of saints and sages from every age, psalms, and suggestions for personal reflection and practice. 6 x 9, 448 pp, Quality PB, 978-1-59473-545-5 **$18.99**
Openings: A Daybook of Saints, Sages, Psalms and Prayer Practices—Leader's Guide
8½ x 11, 12 pp, PB, 978-1-59473-572-1 **$9.99**

Honest to God Prayer: Spirituality as Awareness, Empowerment, Relinquishment and Paradox *By Kent Ira Groff* 6 x 9, 192 pp, Quality PB, 978-1-59473-433-5 **$16.99**

Lectio Divina—The Sacred Art
Transforming Words & Images into Heart-Centered Prayer
By Christine Valters Paintner, PhD 5½ x 8½, 240 pp, Quality PB, 978-1-59473-300-0 **$16.99**
Men Pray: Voices of Strength, Faith, Healing, Hope and Courage
Created by the Editors at SkyLight Paths; With Introductions by Brian D. McLaren
5 x 7¼, 192 pp, HC, 978-1-59473-395-6 **$16.99**

Secrets of Prayer: A Multifaith Guide to Creating Personal Prayer in Your Life
By Nancy Corcoran, CSJ 6 x 9, 160 pp, Quality PB, 978-1-59473-215-7 **$16.99**
Women of Color Pray: Voices of Strength, Faith, Healing, Hope and Courage
Edited and with Introductions by Christal M. Jackson
5 x 7¼, 208 pp, Quality PB, 978-1-59473-077-1 **$15.99**

Prayer / M. Basil Pennington, OCSO

Finding Grace at the Center, 3rd Edition: The Beginning of
Centering Prayer *With Thomas Keating, OCSO, and Thomas E. Clarke, SJ*
Foreword by Rev. Cynthia Bourgeault, PhD A practical guide to a simple and beautiful form of meditative prayer. 5 x 7¼, 128 pp, Quality PB, 978-1-59473-182-2 **$12.99**

The Monks of Mount Athos: A Western Monk's Extraordinary
Spiritual Journey on Eastern Holy Ground *Foreword by Archimandrite Dionysios*
Explores the landscape, monastic communities and food of Athos.
6 x 9, 352 pp, Quality PB, 978-1-893361-78-2 **$18.95**

Psalms: A Spiritual Commentary *Illus. by Phillip Ratner*
Reflections on some of the most beloved passages from the Bible's most widely read book. 6 x 9, 176 pp, 24 full-page b/w illus., Quality PB, 978-1-59473-234-8 **$16.99**

The Song of Songs: A Spiritual Commentary *Illus. by Phillip Ratner*
Explore the Bible's most challenging mystical text. 6 x 9, 160 pp, 14 full-page b/w illus.,
Quality PB, 978-1-59473-235-5 **$16.99** HC, 978-1-59473-004-7 **$19.99**

Women's Interest

There's a Woman in the Pulpit: Christian Clergywomen Share Their Hard Days, Holy Moments & the Healing Power of Humor
Edited by Rev. Martha Spong; Foreword by Rev. Carol Howard Merritt
Offers insight into the lives of Christian clergywomen and the rigors that come with commitment to religious life, representing fourteen denominations as well as dozens of seminaries and colleges. 6 x 9, 240 pp, Quality PB, 978-1-59473-588-2 **$18.99**

She Lives! Sophia Wisdom Works in the World
By Rev. Jann Aldredge-Clanton, PhD
Fascinating narratives of clergy and laypeople who are changing the institutional church and society by restoring biblical female divine names and images to Christian theology, worship symbolism and liturgical language.
6 x 9, 320 pp, Quality PB, 978-1-59473-573-8 **$18.99**

Birthing God: Women's Experiences of the Divine
By Lana Dalberg; Foreword by Kathe Schaaf
Powerful narratives of suffering, love and hope that inspire both personal and collective transformation. 6 x 9, 304 pp, Quality PB, 978-1-59473-480-9 **$18.99**

Women, Spirituality and Transformative Leadership
Where Grace Meets Power
Edited by Kathe Schaaf, Kay Lindahl, Kathleen S. Hurty, PhD, and Reverend Guo Cheen
A dynamic conversation on the power of women's spiritual leadership and its emerging patterns of transformation.
6 x 9, 288 pp, Quality PB, 978-1-59473-548-6 **$18.99**; HC, 978-1-59473-313-0 **$24.99**

Spiritually Healthy Divorce: Navigating Disruption with Insight & Hope
By Carolyne Call A spiritual map to help you move through the twists and turns of divorce. 6 x 9, 224 pp, Quality PB, 978-1-59473-288-1 **$16.99**

Bread, Body, Spirit: Finding the Sacred in Food
Edited and with Introductions by Alice Peck 6 x 9, 224 pp, Quality PB, 978-1-59473-242-3 **$19.99**

Dance—The Sacred Art: The Joy of Movement as a Spiritual Practice
By Cynthia Winton-Henry 5½ x 8½, 224 pp, Quality PB, 978-1-59473-268-3 **$16.99**

Daughters of the Desert: Stories of Remarkable Women from Christian, Jewish and Muslim Traditions *By Claire Rudolf Murphy, Meghan Nuttall Sayres, Mary Cronk Farrell, Sarah Conover and Betsy Wharton*
5½ x 8½, 192 pp, Illus., Quality PB, 978-1-59473-106-8 **$18.99** Inc. reader's discussion guide

The Divine Feminine in Biblical Wisdom Literature
Selections Annotated & Explained
Translation & Annotation by Rabbi Rami Shapiro; Foreword by Rev. Cynthia Bourgeault, PhD
5½ x 8½, 240 pp, Quality PB, 978-1-59473-109-9 **$18.99**

Divining the Body: Reclaim the Holiness of Your Physical Self
By Jan Phillips 8 x 8, 256 pp, Quality PB, 978-1-59473-080-1 **$18.99**

Honoring Motherhood: Prayers, Ceremonies & Blessings
Edited and with Introductions by Lynn L. Caruso
5 x 7¼, 272 pp, Quality PB, 978-1-58473-384-0 **$9.99**; HC, 978-1-59473-239-3 **$19.99**

New Feminist Christianity: Many Voices, Many Views
Edited by Mary E. Hunt and Diann L. Neu
6 x 9, 384 pp, Quality PB, 978-1-59473-435-9 **$19.99**; HC, 978-1-59473-285-0 **$24.99**

Next to Godliness: Finding the Sacred in Housekeeping
Edited by Alice Peck 6 x 9, 224 pp, Quality PB, 978-1-59473-214-0 **$19.99**

The Triumph of Eve & Other Subversive Bible Tales
By Matt Biers-Ariel 5½ x 8½, 192 pp, Quality PB, 978-1-59473-176-1 **$14.99**

Woman Spirit Awakening in Nature: Growing into the Fullness of Who You Are
By Nancy Barrett Chickerneo, PhD; Foreword by Eileen Fisher
8 x 8, 224 pp, b/w illus., Quality PB, 978-1-59473-250-8 **$16.99**

Women of Color Pray: Voices of Strength, Faith, Healing, Hope and Courage
Edited and with Introductions by Christal M. Jackson 5 x 7¼, 208 pp, Quality PB, 978-1-59473-077-1 **$15.99**

Personal Growth

Grieving with Your Whole Heart
Spiritual Wisdom and Practice for Finding Comfort, Hope and Healing after Loss
Created by the Editors at SkyLight Paths; Introduction by Thomas Moore
A spiritual companion that embraces wisdom from across faith traditions to help readers honor, grieve and heal from the losses they face in their lives.
6 x 9, 272 pp, Quality PB, 978-1-59473-599-8 **$18.99**

Forgiving Others, Forgiving Ourselves
Understanding & Healing Our Emotional Wounds
By Myra Warren Isenhart, PhD, and Michael Spangle, PhD
A dynamic look at forgiveness, focusing on heart, mind and soul to discover psychological insights and practical steps to forgive and seek forgiveness.
6 x 9, 160 pp, Quality PB, 978-1-59473-600-1 **$16.99**

Deepening Engagement
Essential Wisdom for Listening and Leading with Purpose, Meaning and Joy
By Diane M. Millis, PhD; Foreword by Rob Lehman
A toolkit for community building as well as a resource for personal growth and small group enrichment.
5 x 7¼, 176 pp, Quality PB, 978-1-59473-584-4 **$14.99**

The Forgiveness Handbook
Spiritual Wisdom and Practice for the Journey to Freedom, Healing and Peace
Created by the Editors at SkyLight Paths; Introduction by The Rev. Canon Marianne Wells Borg
Offers inspiration, encouragement and spiritual practice from across faith traditions for all who seek hope, wholeness and the freedom that comes from true forgiveness. 6 x 9, 256 pp, Quality PB, 978-1-59473-577-6 **$18.99**

Decision Making & Spiritual Discernment
The Sacred Art of Finding Your Way
By Nancy L. Bieber
Presents three essential aspects of Spirit-led decision making: willingness, attentiveness and responsiveness.
5½ x 8½, 208 pp, Quality PB, 978-1-59473-289-8 **$16.99**

Like a Child
Restoring the Awe, Wonder, Joy and Resiliency of the Human Spirit
By Rev. Timothy J. Mooney
Explores Jesus's counsel to become like children in order to enter the kingdom of God. 6 x 9, 160 pp, Quality PB, 978-1-59473-543-1 **$16.99**

Conversation—The Sacred Art
Practicing Presence in an Age of Distraction
By Diane M. Millis, PhD; Foreword by Rev. Tilden Edwards, PhD
5½ x 8½, 192 pp, Quality PB, 978-1-59473-474-8 **$16.99**

Hospitality—The Sacred Art
Discovering the Hidden Spiritual Power of Invitation and Welcome
By Rev. Nanette Sawyer; Foreword by Rev. Dirk Ficca
5½ x 8½, 208 pp, Quality PB, 978-1-59473-228-7 **$16.99**

The Losses of Our Lives
The Sacred Gifts of Renewal in Everyday Loss
By Dr. Nancy Copeland-Payton
6 x 9, 192 pp, Quality PB, 978-1-59473-307-9 **$16.99**; HC, 978-1-59473-271-3 **$19.99**

Secrets of a Soulful Marriage
Creating & Sustaining a Loving, Sacred Relationship
By Jim Sharon, EdD, and Ruth Sharon, MS 6 x 9, 192 pp, Quality PB, 978-1-59473-554-7 **$16.99**

A Spirituality for Brokenness
Discovering Your Deepest Self in Difficult Times
By Terry Taylor 6 x 9, 176 pp, Quality PB, 978-1-59473-229-4 **$16.99**

Spiritual Practice

Dancing Mindfulness
A Creative Path to Healing and Transformation
By Jamie Marich, PhD, LPCC-S; Foreword by Christine Valters Paintner, PhD, Obl. OSB, REACE
A transformative mindfulness-in-motion practice, opening up a creative, embodied way to deepen your spiritual awareness—using dance as the medium of discovery.
6 x 9, 224 pp, Quality PB, 978-1-59473-601-8 **$16.99**

Grieving with Your Whole Heart
Spiritual Wisdom and Practice for Finding Comfort, Hope and Healing after Loss
Created by the Editors at SkyLight Paths; Introduction by Thomas Moore
A spiritual companion that embraces wisdom from across faith traditions to help readers honor, grieve and heal from the losses they face in their lives.
6 x 9, 272 pp, Quality PB, 978-1-59473-599-8 **$18.99**

The Advent of God's Word
Listening for the Power of the Divine Whisper—
A Daily Retreat & Devotional
By Rev. Dr. Brenda K. Buckwell, Obl. OSB
For those who find themselves struggling with no time for prayer during the busy Advent season. Step-by-step creative exercises help you celebrate the birth of Jesus.
6 x 9, 208 pp, Quality PB, 978-1-59473-576-9 **$16.99**

Finding Peace through Spiritual Practice
The Interfaith Amigos' Guide to Personal, Social and Environmental Healing
By Pastor Don Mackenzie, Rabbi Ted Falcon and Imam Jamal Rahman
A look at the specific issues in modern pluralistic society and the spiritual practices that can help transcend roadblocks to effective collaboration on the critical issues of today.
6 x 9, 200 pp (est), Quality PB, 978-1-59473-604-9 **$16.99**

The Forgiveness Handbook
Spiritual Wisdom and Practice for the Journey to Freedom, Healing and Peace
Created by the Editors at SkyLight Paths; Introduction by The Rev. Canon Marianne Wells Borg
Offers inspiration, encouragement and spiritual practice from across faith traditions for all who seek hope, wholeness and the freedom that comes from true forgiveness.
6 x 9, 256 pp, Quality PB, 978-1-59473-577-6 **$18.99**

Fully Awake and Truly Alive
Spiritual Practices to Nurture Your Soul
By Rev. Jane E. Vennard; Foreword by Rami Shapiro
Illustrates the joys and frustrations of spiritual practice across religious traditions; provides exercises and meditations to help you become more fully alive.
6 x 9, 208 pp, Quality PB, 978-1-59473-473-1 **$16.99**

Sacred Attention
A Spiritual Practice for Finding God in the Moment
By Margaret D. McGee
Accessible, humorous and meaningful, these words and practices will lead you further along your path toward discovering a deeper awareness of yourself and your relationship to all that is around you—and within you.
6 x 9, 144 pp, Quality PB, 978-1-59473-291-1 **$16.99**

AVAILABLE FROM BET
TRY YOUR BOOK

About SKYLIGHT PATHS Pu

SkyLight Paths Publishing is creating a
spiritual traditions come together for cl
where we can help each other underst;
heart of our existence.

Through spirituality, our religious beliefs a
our lives—rather than *apart* from our live
interested than ever in spiritual growth,
traditional religion. Yet, we do want to deepen our relationship to the sacred,
to learn from our own as well as from other faith traditions, and to practice
in new ways.

SkyLight Paths sees both believers and seekers as a community that increas-
ingly transcends traditional boundaries of religion and denomination—
people wanting to learn from each other, *walking together, finding the way.*

For your information and convenience, at the back of this book we have
provided a list of other SkyLight Paths books you might find interesting
and useful. They cover the following subjects:

Buddhism / Zen	Gnosticism	Poetry
Catholicism	Hinduism / Vedanta	Prayer
Chaplaincy		Religious Etiquette
Children's Books	Inspiration	Retirement & Later- Life Spirituality
Christianity	Islam / Sufism	
Comparative Religion	Judaism	Spiritual Biography
	Meditation	Spiritual Direction
Earth-Based Spirituality	Mindfulness	Spirituality
	Monasticism	Women's Interest
Enneagram	Mysticism	Worship
Global Spiritual Perspectives	Personal Growth	

Or phone, fax, mail or email to: SKYLIGHT PATHS Publishing
Sunset Farm Offices, Route 4 • P.O. Box 237 • Woodstock, Vermont 05091
Tel: (802) 457-4000 • Fax: (802) 457-4004 • www.skylightpaths.com
Credit card orders: (800) 962-4544 (8:30AM–5:30PM EST Monday–Friday)
Generous discounts on quantity orders. SATISFACTION GUARANTEED. Prices subject to change.

**For more information about each book,
visit our website at www.skylightpaths.com.**

3190 1059713075